Sweet Christmas Cookin'

by

Mary Reynolds Smith

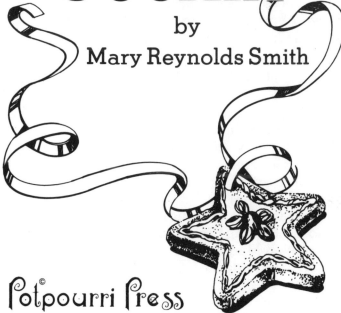

Potpourri Press

Greensboro, North Carolina 27404
Printed in U.S.A.

Table of Contents

Candy

Introduction

When I was a child, Christmas always began at our house on Thanksgiving afternoon when mother baked her holiday fruitcakes.

As soon as Thanksgiving dinner (served at mid-day) was over, our big oak dining room table was cleared, then piled high with all kinds of marvelous ingredients, pans, bowls and utensils. My sister and I were put to work chopping nuts and dicing sticky candied fruits while mother and grandmother measured, mixed, and argued the merits of dark versus light fruitcake family recipes.

Since all the cakes were baked that one day (so they could age gracefully with periodic nips of brandy) and I was young, my bedtime came soon after the first cakes were out of the oven and the last ones were still baking. Consequently, I fell asleep each Thanksgiving with the spicy scent of baking fruitcakes sparking dreams of all the goodies to come before Christmas morning finally dawned.

During the next month, the sweet smell of fruitcake dissolved into a delicious potpourri of other aromas as cakes and cookies baked and candy simmered.

Mother routinely marked all special occasions with something from her kitchen. But Christmas—Christmas was her time, the high point of her year—a magical, marvelous season that offered the supreme opportunity to bake to her heart's content and to share as much as her generous spirit desired.

And there was much to prepare: special treats for the family, some to enjoy at once, others to be carefully packed away for later . . . baskets of goodies to be delivered to neighborhood

4

"shut-ins", the ill and the elderly... extravagant cakes for family dinners and holiday parties... and cookies and candy to be shared with drop-in guests. In addition, there were boxes and boxes of sweets to be packed as gifts for an extraordinary list of people that seemed to grow daily.

Like mother, some people love Christmas and would like for it to last twelve months of the year. Others wish they could ignore it or sleep through it. But—almost everyone spends some time in the kitchen getting ready for it.

For those who enjoy cooking, the holiday season is pure delight. All thoughts of diets vanish and nothing is too sinfully rich or too extravagant to try.

On the other hand, this is the time of year when even the most confirmed "non-cook" feels compelled to whip up a batch of cookies or candy for family and friends.

This book is dedicated to both types. The recipes are varied, some elaborate with long lists of ingredients; others guaranteed to turn out glorious Christmas treats with amazingly little work or expertise.

There are fruitcakes to be given as very special gifts or simply to be enjoyed all through the holidays ... chocolate and coconut and other luscious cakes grand enough to top off traditional family dinners or to star at holiday buffets and other parties.

There are hard-to-resist cookies of all types, some rolled out and cut, some formed, some dropped, others cut into bars or squares—all memorable taste-treats.

And of course there is candy—a variety to suit all tastes. Since many people, even very good cooks, often hesitate to try their hand at candy-making, recipes have been chosen to give the most satisfying results with a minimum of special equipment or experience.

Perhaps so much emphasis is put on cookies and candies because they seem almost synonymous with Christmas and their fragrance conjures up memories of home and childhood and the never-to-be-equaled delights of Christmases-past. On the practical side, such sweet treats provide instant desserts for hastily prepared meals, delicious (and easy) snacks for hectic days and always-ready refreshments for drop-in guests.

Best of all, cookies and candies make marvelous, always-welcome gifts. If you have doubts, try packing tins of them this year for special friends. You'll find they're more than a gift; they quickly become a tradition, a ritual eagerly anticipated by past recipients. Be warned, however, that such giving is so much fun, so self-rewarding, that it becomes addictive. Your list will soon grow, as my mother's always did, to include friends, relatives, teachers, ministers, family doctors and their nurses, the mailman and—nicest of all—the people who've shared a little bit of your life in some special way during the past year, but who never expect to be remembered with a Christmas gift.

This book grew out of the love of holiday baking and delight in sharing the "fruits" of my kitchen that are a precious part of my heritage from my mother. Many of the recipes are gifts from the past, family recipes handed down from grandmother to mother to me (up-dated for today's ingredients and appliances, and carefully kitchen-tested). Others are ones I've added through the years as I've continued the traditional "month of holiday baking".

These treats—cakes, cookies and candies—are always in season, but are perhaps never so special as at Christmas. At no other time will the results taste quite as good or look as pretty. Mother always said this was because we added an extra measure of love and a dash of Christmas magic at this time of year, and perhaps she was right. Certainly, I've never found a better explanation. At any rate, whether you make a few goodies just for the family or a lot to share with friends, you'll find that a little bit of yourself goes into all you make.

Hopefully, some of these recipes will become real favorites of yours, delighting those who share them and becoming a part of your family tradition to be handed down to children of the future . . . a bit of immortality that will bloom again with each new baking. Hopefully, too, the ones you make during the holidays will contain just the right amount of Christmas magic to build lasting memories of delightful taste treats, mixed with love and shared with a generous heart.

Amaretto Trifle Cake

*This is one recipe I can claim as neither "old" nor "family",
but it was given to me by a very special friend, Ruby, and her
husband, are among the truly "generous in spirit" people in
the world, sharing themselves as well as material things with
their friends. Fortunately, that generosity includes sharing
recipes for when they served this for dessert at a special
dinner, I knew I must try it. Ruby, who attributes it to her
daughter-in-law's mother (in the south, family relationships do
tend to get complicated), warned that I might not want it
because it uses a cake mix. She could not have been more
wrong. For this proves what most busy women today know—
that while scratch cooking is great, mixes can be life-savers in
providing the bases for time-saving but marvelous dishes.*

*This has a rich, yet light, taste that compliments a holiday
meal perfectly. And it looks festive, too.*

Preheat oven to 350°. Makes 2 8" layers.

> 1 package (18 1/2 ounces) yellow cake mix
> 1/2 cup corn starch
> 1 cup water
> 4 eggs
> 1/2 cup corn oil
> 1 teaspoon vanilla
> 1/3 cup unsweetened cocoa
> 1/2 cup Amaretto liqueur

Custard Filling and Frosting recipes follow.

Grease and flour two 8" square (or round) pans. In large
mixing bowl, stir together cake mix and corn starch. Add
water, eggs, corn oil and vanilla. Mix at low speed until all
ingredients are moistened. Then beat at medium speed for
three minutes or until batter is smooth. Pour one-half the batter into one of the prepared pans. Sift cocoa over the batter
remaining in the bowl and stir until completely mixed. Pour
into remaining pan and bake 30-35 minutes or until surface
springs back when pressed lightly with fingers. Remove

cakes from over and reduce heat to 300°. Allow layers to cool in pans for 10 minutes. In the meantime, spread almonds for the frosting on cookie sheet and place in oven to toast, stirring occasionally until nuts are golden brown. Remove and set aside to cool. Remove cakes from pans and allow to cool completely. While cake is cooling, prepare custard filling.

CUSTARD FILLING

1/4 cup granulated sugar
1/3 cup corn starch
1/8 teaspoon salt
3 cups milk
4 egg yolks, slightly beaten
1 teaspoon vanilla

In a heavy saucepan, mix together sugar, corn starch and salt. Gradually stir in milk, mixing until smooth. Stir in beaten egg yolks. Over low heat, bring the mixture to a boil and allow to boil for one minute. Remove from heat and stir in vanilla. Cover and refrigerate until chilled.

When ready to assemble the cake, carefully split the layers in half horizontally so that you have four thin layers. Place one chocolate layer on cake plate. Brush with about one-fourth of the 1/2 cup liqueur. Spread with 1/3 of the chilled custard. Repeat process, alternating yellow and chocolate layers. The top layer will be yellow. Brush this with liqueur, but do not spread with custard. Prepare frosting.

FROSTING

2 cups whipping cream
1/4 cup confectioner's sugar
3 tablespoons Amaretto liqueur
1 1-3/4 ounce package slivered
    blanched almonds, toasted

Whip cream until stiff (it is helpful to chill bowl and beaters as well as the cream). Fold in confectioner's sugar and 3 tablespoons liqueur. Frost sides and top of cake. Sprinkle top with toasted almonds and refrigerate until ready to serve.

9

Fresh Apple Spice Cake

This is not a "fancy" cake, but it is a good cake. Good to snack on, good to share with a neighbor over morning coffee on a cold December morning, good for dessert after a simple meal on a busy pre-Christmas day. Tightly covered and stored in a cool place, it keeps several weeks, so you can bake it early. With its apples, nuts and spices, it fills the house with the special smell of holiday baking which may help get you in the mood for more complicated projects, your decorating or gift wrapping. In fact, since it's so easy to make (another "plus" for this recipe), why not make an extra one or two. Keep one at home, share one with a friend or neighbor or take one to the office for a coffee-break holiday surprise.

Preheat oven to 350°. Makes 1 10″ tube pan.

> 3 cups all-purpose flour
> 1 teaspoon baking soda
> 1/4 teaspoon salt
> 1 teaspoon nutmeg
> 1 teaspoon cinnamon
> 1 cup vegetable oil
> 2 cups granulated sugar
> 3 eggs
> 1 teaspoon vanilla
> 1 cup English walnuts or pecans, chopped finely
> 3 cups peeled, finely chopped apples

Glaze recipe follows.

Grease and flour 10″ tube pan and set aside. Sift together the first five ingredients and set aside. Combine oil and sugar and beat well. Add eggs, one at a time, beating well after each addition. Add flour, beating until thoroughly mixed. Add vanilla, pecans and apples and mix well. Pour into tube pan and bake 1 hour, 15 minutes or until cake tester comes out clean. Remove from oven and place on rack (do not turn top side down) while preparing glaze.

GLAZE
1/2 cup granulated sugar
1/4 cup buttermilk
1/4 teaspoon soda
2 tablespoons butter or margarine
1 1/2 teaspoons vanilla

Combine all ingredients in a heavy saucepan and bring to a boil over medium heat. Boil, stirring occasionally, for four minutes. Remove from heat. Using a toothpick, punch holes in the cake while it is still in the pan and still warm. Spoon glaze over it. Allow cake to cool completely on rack before removing it from the pan.

Black Forest Cake

This isn't a family recipe, nor was it one of our holiday traditions. However, the friend who gave me the recipe many years ago said that it was always served on Christmas Eve in her home. I avoided making it for several years because I was "frightened" by the long list of ingredients and apparently complicated assembly. In actuality, it is not a particularly difficult cake to make and is well worth the effort. Once I tried it, it became a favorite to serve at special holiday dinners. And I love serving it when we're having friends just for coffee and dessert. It's a spectacular cake, truly delicious—and besides, doesn't it have a lovely name?

Preheat oven to 350°. Makes 3 8" layers.

BATTER
1/2 cup all-purpose flour
1/2 cup unsweetened cocoa
2/3 cup butter or margarine
6 eggs
1 cup granulated sugar
1/2 teaspoon almond flavoring
1/2 teaspoon vanilla

SYRUP
1/3 cup granulated sugar
1/2 cup water
3 tablespoons Cointreau or other orange liqueur

CHERRY FILLING
1 cup canned dark sweet cherries, pitted
2 tablespoons Cointreau or other orange liqueur
1 tablespoon cornstarch
2/3 cup juice from drained cherries

CREAM FILLING AND FROSTING
3 cups whipping cream, chilled
1/2 cup confectioner's sugar

GARNISH (optional)
Chocolate curls and grated chocolate made from
    1 8-ounce bar dark sweet chocolate

Grease and flour three 8" layer pans. (At this time, it is a good idea to start preparing the cherry filling by combining the cherries with two tablespoons of liqueur and setting it aside to marinate for about an hour. To prepare cake, sift together flour and cocoa and set aside. Melt butter in top of double boiler or in heavy saucepan over very low heat and set aside to cool. In a large bowl, beat eggs until very light in color. Add sugar and continue to beat until mixture is thick (almost the consistency of whipped cream). Add flavoring and mix well. Fold in flour/cocoa mixture alternately with melted butter (do not beat). Spoon into prepared pans and bake 15-18 minutes or until cake tester comes out clean. Turn cakes out of pans onto racks and cool.

While layers are cooling, make syrup by dissolving sugar in water over low heat in heavy saucepan. When sugar is dissolved, bring mixture to a full boil; reduce heat slightly and continue to simmer for 5-6 minutes. Remove from heat and stir in liqueur. Set aside to cool slightly. Meanwhile place cake layers on wax paper covered flat surface and punch several holes in each with a toothpick or your cake tester. When syrup has cooled so that it is only warm to the touch, pour over cake layers and allow to stand while you prepare the cherry and cream fillings.

To make the cherry filling, mix together in heavy saucepan the cornstarch and half the cherry juice. Stir until cornstarch is dissolved. Then stir in the rest of the cherry juice. Place over medium heat and bring to a full boil, stirring almost constantly. Reduce heat and cook for another 3-5 minutes or until mixture is thick and "clear". Remove from heat and allow to cool. Stir in cherries and liqueur and mix together thoroughly.

To prepare cream filling and frosting, beat cream with sugar until it stands in stiff peaks.

To assemble cake, turn one layer over onto cake plate (placing side with holes and syrup mixture down). Spread about 1/2 the cherry mixture over layer and cover with a little less than 1/3 of the whipped cream. Cover with second layer of cake (holes-side down, again). Spread with remaining cherry mixture and then with whipped cream, leaving enough cream to frost the cake. Place the third layer of cake on top (again, holes and syrup side down) and frost sides and top with remaining cream.

To decorate, sprinkle sides and top with grated chocolate. If you wish, prepare chocolate curls and place on center top of cake. To make chocolate curls, shave side of large chocolate bar (8 oz.) with sharp knife or vegetable peeler and place on wax paper in refrigerator until hard. Grate remainder of chocolate bar for garnish.

Chocolate Layer Cake

When I was growing up, this was the birthday cake for everyone in the family (except dad who always got coconut), so even today when I eat chocolate cake, I think of birthdays. However, it's a good holiday cake too because it keeps well (stays nice and moist for several days) and since almost everyone loves chocolate, it's fun to serve most anytime. And, if you need a "family gift" for some friends or neighbors, this cake makes a sure-to-please present. If you're "into" cake decorating, you can do all sorts of things to make it look like a Christmas cake. If—like me—you're not, try sticking a sprig of artificial holly or a toy Santa on top. Or simply wrap it in clear wrap and top with a gay Christmas bow.

This is a big cake, so if it's too much for your family, cut it in half after it's finished. Enjoy one now and save one for later (securely wrapped, it freezes beautifully). Or better still share one half with a busy friend—not as a gift, just a happy holiday gesture.

Preheat oven to 325°. Makes 3 9" layers.

3 cups cake flour
1 1/2 teaspoons baking powder
1 1/2 teaspoons baking soda
3/8 teaspoon salt
3/4 cups butter or margarine
3 cups brown sugar
3 eggs, beaten
3/4 cup milk
3/4 cup sour cream
5 1/2 one-ounce squares
    unsweetened baking chocolate
1 1/2 teaspoons vanilla

Filling and Frosting recipes follow.

Grease and flour pans. Line bottoms with brown paper cut to fit, greased and floured, or with parchment paper.

Sift together the first four ingredients and set aside. Cream butter and 1 1/2 cups of sugar thoroughly. In a separate bowl, beat eggs until light in color. Gradually add the remaining 1 1/2 cups sugar and continue to beat until sugar is well dissolved. Add this to the creamed butter/sugar mixture and continue beating until well mixed (several minutes). In a small bowl, combine milk and sour cream with a small whisk. Add this to batter alternately with flour, mixing well after each addition. Melt chocolate over hot (not boiling) water and add to batter along with vanilla and beat well.

Pour into prepared pans and bake 25-30 minutes or until surface springs back when pressed lightly, or cake tester comes out clean. Allow to cool for several minutes on rack; then turn layers out of pan and cool completely on rack before filling and frosting.

FILLING
1 cup butter or margarine
8 cups confectioner's sugar
4 teaspoons lemon juice
4 tablespoons strong coffee
2 cups pecans, ground very finely

Cream butter thoroughly. Add approximately one half the confectioner's sugar, continuing to beat vigorously. Add lemon juice and coffee and beat well. Add remaining confectioner's sugar and beat until well mixed. Add finely ground nuts and mix thoroughly. Spread between layers of cake.

FUDGE FROSTING
6 tablespoons butter or margarine
1 1/2 tablespoons light corn syrup
3 1-ounce squares unsweetened baking chocolate
1/2 cup milk
1 1/2 cups granulated sugar
1/8 teaspoon salt
1 1/2 teaspoons vanilla

Combine all ingredients, except vanilla, in a heavy saucepan and bring to a rolling boil over medium heat. Continue to boil, stirring constantly for one minute. Remove from heat and cool. Add vanilla and beat at high speed until mixture is thick and glossy. Spread on sides and top of cake at once.

Fresh Coconut Cake

Fresh coconut cake was a "must" to be served sometime during our family's holiday season—partly because it was good and pretty, but mostly because it was my father's favorite cake. Mother always made it for his birthday, and he insisted on calling it his "birthday cake" regardless of when it was served. It was strictly mother's specialty. My only participation was hand-grating the coconut (and sometimes my fingertips), and it was one of the few things baked in our kitchen that I never learned to make. Mother baked it from memory or by instinct (certainly not from written instructions), and after her death, I finally gave up trying to duplicate it. Then I married and acquired a very special sister-in-law, Carrie, who baked a fresh coconut cake that tasted just like mother's. She, too, baked by instinct, but over the years with her help, I translated her "little of this" and "dash of that" into a recipe I could follow. While to me, my cake never really measures up to those baked by these two remarkable women, the following is quite good and is sure to win compliments for you.

Preheat oven to 325°. Makes 3 9" layers.

- 1 cup butter
- 2 cups sugar
- 4 eggs, separated
- 3 cups cake flour
- 3 teaspoons baking powder
- 1 teaspoon salt
- 1 cup milk
- 1 teaspoon vanilla

Filling and Frosting recipes follow.

Grease and flour three 9" layer pans. Cut brown paper to fit bottoms of pan and grease and flour paper or use parchment cut to fit.

Cream butter and sugar together thoroughly. Add egg yolks one at a time, beating well after each addition. Sift together flour, baking powder and salt. Add this, alternately with milk, mixing well after each addition. In a separate bowl, beat egg whites until they are stiff, but not dry. Fold egg whites into batter, blending completely. Add vanilla, mixing well. Pour into prepared pans and bake 25-30 minutes or until surface springs back when pressed gently (or until cake tester comes out clean). Cool completely on rack. Put together with filling and cover with cooked frosting.

COCONUT CAKE FILLING

2 cups granulated sugar
1 1/2 cups coconut milk*
3 1/2 cups grated fresh coconut

To prepare the fresh coconut, pierce two or three holes in the "eye" end of the coconut and drain the milk. Reserve. To open the coconut, wrap it in a heavy cloth and tap it several different places with a hammer until it cracks and you can pull away the heavy husk. An easier way is to place it in a preheated (to 325°) oven for 15 minutes. Remove; wrap in heavy cloth and tap with a hammer. The coconut will break more easily and the husk will fall away with less effort on your part. With a sharp knife, pare away the thin brown skin and then either hand grate the meat or cut it into small pieces and process in blender or food processor.

Combine sugar and coconut milk in a heavy saucepan and bring to a boil. Reduce heat and simmer for 10 minutes. Remove from heat and stir in coconut. Spread, in equal parts, between layer of cake. Frost sides and top with the following.

COOKED FROSTING

2 cups granulated sugar
1/4 cup white Karo syrup
1/4 cup water
2 egg whites
1 cup grated coconut (optional)

Combine sugar, syrup and water in heavy saucepan and cook over medium heat until mixture looks clear. Meanwhile beat 2 egg whites until they stand in stiff peaks. Pour 6 table-spoons of the hot liquid slowly over the egg whites, beating constantly until the mixture is cool. Meanwhile, continue cooking sugar syrup until candy thermometer registers 260°

(or hard ball stage). Remove from heat and pour very slowly over egg white mixture, beating constantly until mixture is shiny and of spreading consistency. Frost sides and top of cake. Using hands, pat coconut over sides and top for the finishing touch.

*If you do not have sufficient milk from your coconut, complete the amount called for with coconut milk prepared the following way. Using 1 cup fresh grated coconut or 1 cup of packaged flaked coconut, pour over it 1 cup scalded milk. Allow to soak for 15-20 minutes and strain. Refrigerate milk until ready to use.

Chocolate Fruitcake

Fruitcake baking was a tradition in my family, but mother and grandmother could never agree on the best recipe. Grandmother mixed the dark chocolate cake she'd made since she was a young girl (and candied her own fruit), while mother preferred the light fruitcake that my father liked. We children were wise enough not to voice a preference, but secretly felt that grandmother's cake was a little extra-special because it included chocolate. Today, I still like the dark richness chocolate lends to the cake, and once you try it, you may find it becomes a tradition in your family, too. Be sure, however, to bake it early (1 to 2 months before Christmas) for proper aging.

Preheat oven to 200°.

Makes 1 10" tube pan plus any one of the following combinations

> 2-9" x 5" loaf pans or
> 2-6" x 5" x 4" foil bakers* or
> 4-4" square foil bakers*

Foil Bakers are available in many stores or they may be ordered from Potpourri Press, P.O. Box 10312, Greensboro, N.C. 27404. Send $2.50 (includes postage and handling) for each set of four 4" bakers or each set of two 6" bakers.

1 pound butter or margarine, softened
1 pound dark brown sugar
12 large eggs
3 1/2 cups all-purpose flour
1 teaspoon baking powder
2 teaspoons cinnamon
1 teaspoon mace
1/2 teaspoon ground cloves
1/4 cup brandy
4 ounces bittersweet chocolate, melted and
  cooled
1 pound seedless raisins
1 pound currants
1 pound candied cherries, cut into pieces
1 1/2 pounds candied pineapple, coarsely diced
1/2 pound citron, diced
1/4 pound candied lemon rind, diced
1/4 pound candied orange rind, diced
1 pound pecans, coarsely chopped
1 pound English walnuts, coarsely chopped
1 1/2 cups all-purpose flour

Grease tube pan and 9" loaf pans and line bottoms with geased brown paper or with parchment. If using smaller foil loaf pans, grease or spray with vegetable shortening spray.

Cream butter until light in color. Add sugar and continue to mix until thoroughly creamed. Add eggs one at a time, beating well after each addition. Sift 3 1/2 cups of flour with baking powder and spices and add to batter, mixing well. Blend in brandy and melted chocolate.

Combine fruits and nuts in large bowl and add 1 1/2 cups flour, mixing with hands until all flour is used and fruits and nuts are well coated. Add to cake batter and mix thoroughly.

Pour into prepared pans and bake for the following lengths of time, or until cake tester comes out clean: tube pan, 2 hours, 45 minutes; 9" loaf pan, 2 hours, 15 minutes; 6" loaf pan, 2 hours, 15 minutes; 4" loaf pan, 1 hour, 15 minutes.

When cakes are done, allow to cool on racks in pans. Remove and wrap each cake in brandy soaked cheesecloth or other soft cloth. Wrap in foil or plastic wrap or place in tightly covered tins. Store in cool place, adding a bit of brandy to the cloth every week or ten days to age the cakes properly.

Traditional Dark Fruitcake

Occasionally, as an alternative to grandmother's chocolate fruitcake, mother made a more traditional dark fruitcake which has been one of my stand-bys for years.

Preheat oven to 325°.

Makes 1 10" tube cake pan or 2 9"x 4" loaf pans or 4 4" square Foil Bakers.*

> 1 cup butter or margarine
> 2 cups brown sugar
> 2 teaspoons lemon flavoring
> 4 eggs
> 3/4 cup molasses
> 4 cups all-purpose flour
> 1 teaspoon baking soda
> 2 teaspoons cinnamon
> 1 teaspoon allspice
> 1 teaspoon mace
> 1 teaspoon ground cloves
> 1 teaspoon salt
> 1/2 cup sour cream
> 1/2 cup brandy
> 1 1/4 cups candied cherries, chopped
> 1 1/4 cups candied pineapple, chopped
> 1 1/3 cups candied citron, chopped
> 1/3 cup candied orange peel,
>   finely chopped
> 1/3 cup candied lemon peel,
>   finely chopped
> 3/4 cup currants
> 1 cup seedless raisins
> 2 cups pecans, chopped
> 1 cup almonds, chopped

Grease and flour tube pan and loaf pans and line bottoms with brown paper, cut to fit, and greased and floured or a double layer of parchment cut to fit. If using the Foil Bakers, grease lightly or spray with vegetable oil spray.

Cream butter thoroughly and add brown sugar, continuing to beat until completely blended. Add lemon flavoring and eggs and beat well. Add molasses and blend thoroughly. Sift 3 1/4 cups flour with soda, salt and spices and set aside. Blend sour cream and brandy with a small wire whisk. Add to batter alternately with flour and mix thoroughly. Mix the remaining 3/4 cup of flour with fruit and nuts, being sure pieces are completely coated. Add to batter, mixing completely. Pour into prepared pans. Bake tube pan 3 hours, 9"x4" loaf pans 2 hours, 30 minutes and small Foil Bakers 2 hours to 2 hours, 15 minutes. Partially cool on rack before removing from pans. Carefully peel off paper and allow cakes to cool completely. (If baking in Foil Bakers, cakes will slip out when cool. Save bakers if you wish to put cakes back in them before putting them into the tins). Wrap cakes in brandy-soaked soft cloth and wrap in aluminum foil or plastic wrap or place in airtight container and store in cool place. Unwrap and add brandy to the cakes every week or ten days until ready to use.

*Folding Foil Bakers are available in many stores. They are also available by mail. See note on page 18.

Ice Box Fruitcake

The first time I tasted this was in the late 1940's when television was still a novelty in our area. The recipe was featured on a local cooking program and mother, who loved trying a new recipe as much as I still do, tried it at once. But, as usual, added her own variations. It was an instant success with the family and continued to be a favorite throughout our "growing up" years.

Even though I hadn't eaten it in years, when I started collecting recipes for this book, it was one of the first holiday favorites I remembered and I started looking, unsuccessfully, for our old recipe. In my frustration, I mentioned it to a sister-in-law who said her mother had made a similar cake years ago and she'd aşk about it. Her mother "Aunt Sally", who is a remarkable and delightfully charming lady of some 90-plus years, produced her recipe about the same time I unearthed mother's. They were quite similar and, after a little experimentation, I ended up with a combination of the two that passed taste-testing by my family and friends.

The experience re-kindled almost forgotten memories of mother mixing it and allowing us the first taste as she packed it into loaf pans, and how good it was to us. However, the cake is better after it has been refrigerated for a week and then it will keep almost indefinitely. The cakes make nice—and a bit unusual—gifts, too. But do enclose a note saying that it needs to be kept refrigerated. And if you're giving it to another "cook", be extra generous and include the recipe.

Makes 2-9"x5" loaf pans or 4-4" square Foil Bakers* plus 12 miniature cupcakes.

> 1 16-ounce box graham crackers
> 1 cup seedless white raisins
> 1 9-ounce package chopped dates
> 1 pound candied cherries, chopped
> 1 pound pecans, broken into pieces
> 1 pound English walnuts, broken into pieces
> 1 cup flaked or grated coconut (optional)
> 1 13-ounce can condensed milk
> 1 16-ounce package marshmallows

To prepare loaf pans, line with two strips of aluminum foil, one lengthwise and one crosswise, allowing each to extend far enough to provide a cover for the cake when it is folded down. This will also help remove cake from pan for slicing. If you're making miniature cupcakes (and if you're doing these primarily for gifts, you may wish to make the whole recipe into these attractive small cakes), use small foil liners in the pans and pack cake mixture directly into them. After cupcakes become firm, they can be removed from pans and packed in tins in layers separated by wax paper and returned to the refrigerator.

To prepare the batter, put graham crackers in blender or food processor and process until fine. Combine in large bowl with raisins, dates, cherries, nuts and coconut. Heat milk in a heavy saucepan over medium heat (do not boil). Add marshmallows and stir until melted and mixture is smooth. A stir or two with a wire whisk is helpful in getting the mixture smooth. Pour over graham cracker/fruit/nut combination and mix together thoroughly. (This is very thick and stiff and I find it easier to work with my hands to completely mix it.) Pack firmly into prepared pans, cover and refrigerate until ready to use. *Folding 4" Foil Bakers are available in many stores, or may be purchased by mail. See note on page 18.*

1997 Xmas
Very good

White Fruitcake ✓

My dad had always refused to eat fruitcake until he tasted mother's white fruitcake. That he liked and that she made every year. While you may think nothing can replace your traditional dark fruitcake, I hope you'll try this lighter version for a very pleasant change.

This cake has a big advantage, too. While it keeps well and ages beautifully wrapped in a brandy-soaked cloth, it's good as soon as it's cool enough to cut (though you really should try to let it "rest" overnight). So it's great for those years when mid-December finds you with your holiday fruitcakes still unbaked.

Preheat oven to 275°. Makes 1-10" tube or 2 -9"x4" loaf pans.

- 1 1/2 pounds almonds, blanched, slivered or chopped (approximately 5 cups)
- 3/4 pound candied pineapple, chopped (2 cups)
- 3/4 pound candied cherries, chopped (2 cups)
- 3/4 pound white raisins (2 cups)
- 4 cups sifted all-purpose flour
- 1/2 teaspoon baking soda
- 1 teaspoon baking powder
- 1 1/2 cups butter or margarine
- 2 cups granulated sugar
- 6 eggs, separated
- 1 teaspoon cream of tartar
- 1/3 cup sour cream
- 1/3 cup brandy
- 2 teaspoons almond flavoring

Prepare pans by greasing and flouring. Line bottom with brown paper, cut to fit and then greased and floured. Or line with parchment.

To blanch almonds, drop in boiling water for several seconds, transfer to cold water and slip brown skins off by rubbing nuts between your fingers. Chop almonds, pineapple, and cherries into desired size pieces. Combine with raisins and 3/4 cup flour, mixing to be sure all fruits and nuts are completely coated with flour. Set aside.

Sift remaining flour with soda and baking powder and set aside. Cream butter well. Add sugar gradually, continuing to cream until thoroughly mixed. In a separate bowl, beat egg yolks and add to butter/sugar mixture, beating thoroughly. Stir together sour cream, brandy and almond flavoring with a wire whisk. Add to batter alternately with sifted flour, mixing well. Fold in flour-coated fruits and nuts and mix thoroughly. In a separate bowl, beat egg whites until they are foamy. Add cream of tartar and continue beating until they stand in stiff peaks. Fold egg whites into batter and pour into prepared pans. Bake tube pan 2 hours, 30 minutes and bake loaf pan 2 hours, or until cake tester comes out clean. Cool on rack for about half an hour. Turn cakes out of pan; remove paper and store in airtight container in cool place. If not using within several days, wrap in brandy-soaked soft cloth, then wrap in aluminum or plastic wrap or put in tightly covered container. Add a bit of brandy every week or so to insure moistness.

Lane Cake

This cake was served only at our most special holiday meal each year and its appearance at the table was always preceded by the announcement, "Here's grandmother Lane's cake". At least I thought that's what mother was saying and I thought it was because my grandmother, whose family name was Lane, always made it. Not so! What my mother was really saying was "here's grandmother's Lane Cake". And as I began to grow up and read and collect cookbooks, I found references to the Lane Cake in one version or another in various family recipe collections and regional cookbooks. No one seems to know the origin of the name, but while that may be in doubt, the goodness of the cake is not, and I urge you to try it—whatever your family name may be. As for me, it will always be a little extra-special because it brings with each year's baking fresh memories of my own grandmother Lane.

Preheat oven to 375°. Makes 3-9" layers.

> 1 cup butter or margarine, softened
> 2 cups granulated sugar
> 1 teaspoon vanilla
> 3 1/2 cups cake flour
> 4 teaspoons baking powder
> 1/2 teaspoon salt
> 1 cup milk
> 1 cup egg whites (usually 7 or 8 eggs)

Filling recipe follows. Frosting recipe (optional) on page 17.

Grease and flour pans thoroughly and set aside. Cream butter and sugar together until light and fluffy. Add vanilla and continue to beat for about another minute. Sift together flour, baking powder and salt. Add to batter, alternately with milk, beating thoroughly after each addition. In a separate bowl, beat egg whites until they stand in stiff peaks when mixer is lifted. Fold egg whites into batter, blending thoroughly. Pour into prepared pans and bake 25 minutes or until surface springs back when pressed gently, or cake tester comes out clean. Cool on rack in pans for 10-15 minutes. Turn cakes out of pan and allow to cool completely on racks before filling and frosting.

FILLING

1/2 cup butter or margarine
6 egg yolks
3/4 cup granulated sugar
1/8 teaspoon salt
2 cups raisins, ground
1 cup grated coconut
3 cups pecans, finely chopped
1/4 cup brandy
1/2 teaspoon vanilla

Melt butter in top of double boiler. In a large bowl, beat egg yolks with sugar and salt until very light in color. Add to butter and continue cooking until mixture thickens. In a separate bowl, combine raisins, coconut, pecans, brandy and vanilla. Pour cooked mixture over this and mix thoroughly. Allow to cool slightly and spread between layers of cake as you assemble it. If you wish, save enough to spread on the top and leave the cake unfrosted. There are those, including my grandmother, who insisted that this was the original version of the Lane Cake and that it needed no frosting.

However, there are many people who prefer to use all the filling between the layers and frost the sides and top with a cooked icing, both because it's pretty and because they like the combination of flavors. If you wish to frost the cake, your own favorite cooked icing will be fine. Or we suggest using the one on page 17, simply eliminating the coconut. Swirl the frosting on sides and top of cake, and if you are serving it during the holidays, you may wish to add a wreath design on top of candied red and green pineapple and cherries.

Pecan Bourbon Cake

When I discovered that the man I married didn't like fruit-cake, I began a search, without much success, for a Christmas cake that would appeal to him and still have the fragrance and aging qualities of the traditional fruitcake. Then one holiday, we had dinner with one of my oldest and dearest friends who is, incidentally, also an excellent cook. For dessert, she served this cake and my husband loved it. My friend Jackie gave me her recipe and it soon became one of my holiday favorites. Bake it early because, while it is good almost as soon as it is cool enough to cut, it is even better after it has aged, wrapped in a brandy-soaked cloth. Baked in a tube pan and decorated with candied fruits, it will grace any holiday table. Baked in small loaf pans, the recipe will give you several truly spectacular gifts.

Preheat oven to 275°. Makes 1-10"tube pan and 1-9"x5" loaf pan or 6-4"x4" Foil Bakers.*

   2 cups candied cherries, cut in halves or quarters
   2 cups seedless white raisins
   2 cups bourbon
   2 cups butter or margarine
   2 1/4 cups granulated sugar
   1 3/4 cups packed light brown sugar
   8 eggs, separated
   5 cups all-purpose flour
   1 1/2 teaspoons baking powder
   1/2 teaspoon salt
   2 1/4 teaspoons ground nutmeg
   4 cups pecans (in halves, or broken coarsely)
   Candied fruit for decoration (optional)

Combine cherries, raisins and bourbon in a bowl. Cover tightly and allow to stand in refrigerator overnight.

On the following day, grease and flour tube pan and loaf pan, lining bottom with greased and floured brown paper cut to fit or a double layer of parchment. If using small foil loaf pans*, grease and flour or spray with vegetable oil spray.

Drain fruits that have been marinating in the refrigerator and reserve bourbon. In a separate bowl, combine 3/4 cup flour with pecans, stirring to be sure nuts are thoroughly coated, and set aside.

In large bowl, beat butter until it is light and fluffy. Add sugar gradually, continuing to beat at medium speed until thoroughly mixed. Add egg yolks one at a time, beating well after each addition. Sift 4 1/4 cups flour with baking powder, salt and nutmeg. Add 2 cups of the flour to batter and mix thoroughly. Add the remainder of the flour and the reserved bourbon alternately, mixing well. In another bowl, beat egg whites until they form stiff peaks when mixer is lifted. Fold egg whites into cake batter gently and blend completely. Finally fold in drained fruits and floured nuts and mix thoroughly.

Fill tube pan to within 1" of top of pan and pour remaining batter into 9" x 5" loaf pan. Bake large cake approximately 3 hours and loaf pan one hour and a half, or until cake tester comes out clean. Bake small loaves one hour and a half or until cake tester comes out clean. (Note: The batter can be baked in paper-lined cupcake pans which, packed in tins, make marvelous gifts. When baking cupcakes, reduce baking time to 35-40 minutes.)

Cool cakes on rack before removing from pans. Peel off paper and wrap each cake in cheesecloth or other soft cloth saturated with bourbon or brandy. Wrap in aluminum foil or plastic wrap or in a tightly covered container and store in a cool place. Add a dose of brandy or bourbon every week or ten days until ready to use.

*4" folding Foil Bakers are available in many stores. They are also available by mail. See note on page 18.

Pound Cake

As long as she was able to bake, when grandmother made pound cake, she used the recipe which gave the cake its name—a pound of butter, a pound of sugar, etc. Mother, however, baked a lighter and, to me, better textured and tasting version—the one I still use. I seldom bake it, however, without remembering mother, as she put hers into the oven, warning her rowdy children not to run and slam the door or the cake would "fall" and have a "sad" or heavy streak. So even now, I check the progress of my pound cake only when it is almost done and then I open and shut the oven door very carefully.

While it's certainly not strictly a holiday cake, a pound cake is very comforting to have on hand during the busy Christmas season because, sliced thinly, it is always delicious and can be served almost anytime with anything.

Makes 1-9"tube pan.

2 cups all-purpose flour
1/4 teaspoon nutmeg
1 teaspoon mace
1/2 teaspoon salt
1 cup butter, softened
1 3/4 cups granulated sugar, sifted
5 eggs

Grease and flour pan and set aside. Sift together the first four ingredients and set aside. Allow butter to soften and then cream well, beating for several minutes. Add sifted sugar gradually, beating thoroughly. Add eggs, one at a time, beating well after each addition. Add flour and beat thoroughly. Pour into prepared pan and place in cold oven. set heat at 300° and bake 1 hour, 45 minutes to 2 hours or until a cake tester comes out clean. Cool on rack for about 10 minutes before turning cake out of pan and allowing to cool completely on rack.

Notes on Cookie Baking

*The first and most fundamental rule of cookie baking is—
enjoy yourself.*

*There are a number of "fun things" about baking cookies.
Unlike a cake, which when finished, must remain untouched
until you're ready to serve it, cookies can be tasted immediately (may not be so good for the figure, but tremendously
satisfying for the cook). Also a platter of cookies, fresh from
the oven, delights almost everyone.*

*And baking cookies is just so ego-satisfying. You may not
be a fantastic cook, but somehow you feel like one when you
look at a platter of fresh-from-the-oven cookies. And you'll
find cookie baking easy if you follow a few simple rules.*

*First, have the equipment you need gathered together and
readily available. This includes heavy baking sheets (it's helpful to have several, but you can get by with only one), aluminum foil, wax paper, a mixer or rotary beater, mixing spoons,
a set of accurate measuring cups and spoons, a wire rack for
cooling cookies, and plenty of working space.*

*Be sure to follow the recipes. Measure all ingredients
accurately (remembering that measurements are level unless otherwise specified). And if you're not sure of your oven
temperature, it's helpful to invest in an inexpensive oven
thermometer so you can check and be sure that it is accurate,
or, if not, you can adjust for it.*

*Lining your baking sheets with aluminum foil or parch-
ment eliminates lots of clean-up time, saves your having to
grease and re-grease cookie sheets and often saves time in
baking because you can slide one sheet of just baked cookies
onto a rack to cool and slide on another sheet filled with
ready-to-bake cookies and put them right into the oven.*

*But remember, baking cookies, while not complicated, is
time-consuming, so allow yourself a comfortable amount of
time to devote to the job, so you can enjoy it. And last of all—
experiment if you feel like it. Who knows? The variation you
come up with may turn out to be the family favorite.*

Happy cookie baking and happy holidays—all year round!

Almond Pretzels

While these are marvelous "companion" cookies for the chocolate pretzels on page 43, they are good enough and pretty enough to serve or give away all by themselves. They keep up to ten days in a tightly covered container so they can be made early in the holiday season—a fact that is especially nice since they definitely take longer to make than drop or rolled-and-cut cookies. But they are also definitely worth the time!

Preheat oven to 350°. Makes approximately 4 dozen.

1 3/4 cups all-purpose flour
1/2 teaspoon baking powder
1/2 teaspoon cinnamon
1/2 teaspoon grated lemon rind
1/2 cup butter or margarine
1/2 cup granulated sugar
2 tablespoons sour cream
1 teaspoon almond extract
3 eggs
1 teaspoon water
1/2 cup finely ground blanched almonds
1/8 cup granulated sugar

Sift together the first four ingredients and set aside. Cream butter and add sugar gradually, continuing to cream until mixture is almost white in color. Add two eggs, sour cream and flavoring and mix well. Add flour and spices and mix thoroughly. Chill dough for several hours until it is manageable.

When ready to bake, grease and lightly flour cookie sheet. Beat together the remaining egg and water in a small bowl and set aside. Grind almonds or process in blender or food processor, mixed with the sugar until very fine. Set aside.

Follow directions on page 43 for forming the pretzels. Brush the tops with egg and sprinkle with almond/sugar mixture. Place about 1" apart on baking sheet and bake for 12-15 minutes. Cool on rack and store tightly covered.

Amaretti

For many years, I have been absolutely addicted to those marvelously crisp imported Italian Amaretti. I love everyting about them—the taste, the crunch, the way they're wrapped in interesting pastel tissues and packed in a bright tin covered with Italian words I can't read. Knowing there were only a few ingredients in the cookies, I was sure that I could duplicate them easily. I couldn't. But after many attempts, with results ranging from too-hard to too-chewy, I reached the following satisfactory combination of ingredients. They taste, I think, as do most homemade goodies, better than the ones you buy. Tightly covered, they keep for weeks and make superior gifts for very, very dear people. For a special touch, try wrapping two cookies, flat sides together, in bits of colorful Christmas tissue before packing them in gift tins.

Preheat oven to 375°. Makes approximately 5 dozen.

> 1 pound almonds
> 1 1/2 cups granulated sugar
> 1 heaping teaspoon confectioner's sugar
> 2/3 cup egg whites (4 to 5)
> 2 teaspoons almond extract

Put almonds into boiling water and leave for approximately 45 seconds. Drain, rinse in cold water and rub between fingers to remove brown skin. Dry on a paper towel and then place on a foil lined cookie sheet in the 375° oven for about 3 minutes. Remove and allow to cool completely. Combine almonds, 1 1/4 cups sugar, and confectioner's sugar in blender or food processor fitted with metal blade and process until very fine. In a large mixing bowl, beat egg whites until they form stiff peaks. Blend in almond/sugar mixture and almond extract, mixing thoroughly by hand until a smooth paste-like dough is formed. With a pastry tube, teaspoon or melon-ball scoop, form balls approximately 1" in diameter and place on lightly greased and floured cookie sheet 2" apart. Sprinkle with remaining granulated sugar. Bake 15-20 minutes until well browned. Remove cookies to a rack with a spatula and allow to cool completely before packing in tightly covered container.

Apple Spice Delights

This was a cake that turned into cookies. I had started to make a fresh apple cake and discovered I only had two apples. Remembering that sometime before my husband Clay, who loves apple-anything, had asked during one of my cookie baking sprees why I never made apple cookies, I decided to turn my cake into cookies. They were easy, moist, almost universally popular. They keep well, tightly covered, and stored in a cool place. The glaze adds sweetness and perhaps makes the cookies look a bit prettier, but I think I like them best without it. I leave that up to your particular taste preference.

Preheat oven to 375°. Makes 6 dozen.

> 2 1/4 cups all-purpose flour
> 1 teaspoon baking powder
> 1 1/4 teaspoon cinnamon
> 1 1/4 teaspoon ground nutmeg
> 1/2 cup butter or margarine
> 1 1/3 cups light brown sugar, firmly packed
> 1 1/4 cups peeled and finely chopped apple
>   (1 large or 2 small)
> 1 cup raisins, chopped
> 1 cup pecans or walnuts, finely chopped
> 1/4 cup apple juice
> 1 tsp. grated lemon rind (optional)

Glaze (optional) to follow.

Sift together the first four ingredients and set aside. Cream butter and add sugar, continuing to mix until light in appearance. Add apples, raisins, nuts, apple juice and lemon rind and mix thoroughly. Add flour and mix well. Chill for 15 minutes. Using a teaspoon, drop in mounds on greased cookie sheet, about 2" apart. Bake 12-15 minutes. Remove to rack to cool. If using a glaze, dip tops of cookies in glaze while still slightly warm and return to rack to dry and cool completely before storing. Store in tightly covered container in cool place.

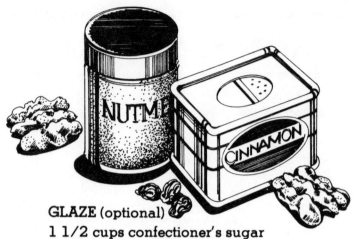

GLAZE (optional)
1 1/2 cups confectioner's sugar
1 tablespoon butter or margarine
3 tablespoons apple juice

Combine all ingredients and beat until smooth. Dip tops of warm cookies in glaze and allow to drip, dry and completely cool on rack. If cookies become completely cool, brush glaze on tops with a pastry brush.

Apricot Pastry Triangles

There may be a better combination of flavors than sweet apricots, almonds and pastry, but it's difficult for me to imagine one, so naturally this recipe is one of my favorites. Besides, the dainty triangles look pretty on a tea table or in a gift tin.

They keep well, tightly covered, for several days, but are really better fresh, so leave this project for one of your last "baking days" before Christmas.

Preheat oven to 350°. Makes approximately 80.

PASTRY
1 cup butter or margarine
1/2 pound cream cheese
1/4 teaspoon salt
2 cups all-purpose flour

FILLING

1 1/4 cups apricot preserves

TOPPING

2 egg whites
1/2 cup finely ground almonds
1/4 cup granulated sugar, sifted

To prepare pastry, allow cream cheese and butter to soften at room temperature. Sift together flour and salt and set aside. Cream butter and cream cheese together. Add flour and cream until thoroughly mixed. Divide in four equal parts, wrap in clear wrap and chill for several hours.

Working with one-fourth of the pastry at a time, roll on floured surface and cut into 2"-2 1/2" squares. (A diamond-shaped cookie cutter or the lid of a small square tin works fine. Otherwise, simply measure and cut squares approximate size you want.) Put 1/2 to 3/4 of a teaspoonful of apricot preserves in center and bring edges together to form a triangle. Press edges together with tines of fork dipped in flour or granulated sugar. Prick tops with fork.

For topping, beat egg whites until they are foamy. Mix together finely ground almonds and sugar or process them together in your blender or food processor. Brush tops of triangles with egg white and sprinkle with nut mixture. Place on greased and lightly floured cookie sheet about 1" apart and bake 15-18 minutes until very lightly browned. Cool on rack and pack in tightly covered containers, in layers separated by waxed paper.

Camel Cookies

*I'm not sure what the original name of these cookies might
have been, (perhaps "date/nut surprises"), but children inevitably describe them as "camel cookies" because of the hump
in the middle and so in our house they've been called Camel
Cookies for many years. As you may gather, they're a funny
looking cookie, but so good they don't have to be pretty.*

Preheat oven to 400°. Makes approximately 36.

> 1 8 ounce package pitted dates
>   (approximately 36 dates)
> 36 walnut or pecan halves (or enough
>   to fill all the dates)
> 1/3 cup butter or margarine
> 3/4 cup brown sugar, firmly packed
> 1 egg
> 1 teaspoon vanilla
> 1 1/2 cups flour
> 1/2 teaspoon salt
> 1/2 teaspoon soda
> 1/4 teaspoon baking powder
> 1/2 cup sour cream

Lightly grease cookie sheet or spray with vegetable oil
spray or line sheet with foil or parchment.

Stuff dates with walnut or pecan halves, press closed firmly and set aside.

Cream butter well. Add sugar gradually, continuing to cream until well mixed. Add egg and vanilla and beat thoroughly. Sift together flour, salt, soda, and baking powder. Add about one-half dry mixture to batter, mixing well. Beat in one-half the sour cream, mixing well. Repeat with remaining flour and sour cream. For each cookie, drop about a level teaspoonful of batter on prepared cookie sheet; place date in center and put a scant teaspoon of batter on top, smoothing it over the date to completely cover it. Place cookies about 2 1/2" apart. Bake 10-12 minutes. Cool on rack and store in tightly covered container in cool place.

Caramel Spritz Cookies

This is a good basic cookie, crispy with a bit of a caramel taste. Since you really do need to use a cookie press, you can turn out a variety of shapes quickly and easily; they keep well, in a tightly covered container and almost everyone likes them.

Preheat oven to 375°. Makes 8 dozen.

> 2 1/4 cups all-purpose flour
> 1/4 teaspoon salt
> 1 cup butter or margarine
> 1/2 cup brown sugar, firmly packed
> 1 egg
> 1 teaspoon vanilla or maple flavoring

Sift together the flour and salt and set aside. Cream butter thoroughly and gradually add sugar, continuing to beat until well mixed. Add egg and flavoring, beating well: then blend in flour and mix well. Using a cookie press, make cookies desired shapes and place on lightly greased or foil-lined cookie sheet about 2" apart. Bake 8-10 minutes or until very lightly browned. Slide from cookie sheet to wire rack immediately and allow to cool completely before storing in tightly covered container.

Chocolate Bars

A cross between a brownie, a cake square and a candy bar, these are popular with almost everyone (especially little boys of all ages) unless they're allergic to chocolate.

They're easy to make and keep up to 2 weeks, tightly covered. They also pack and travel well, so they're a good choice for far-away friends.

Preheat oven to 350°. Makes approximately 4 dozen small squares.

> 1/2 cup butter or margarine, softened
> 1 cup sugar
> 1 16-ounce can chocolate syrup
> 4 eggs
> 1 cup flour
> 1 teaspoon baking powder
> 1 teaspoon vanilla
> 48 pecan halves (optional)

ICING

> 1/2 cup butter or margarine
> 1 cup sugar
> 4 tablespoons cream or condensed milk
> 1/2 cup chocolate bits, milk chocolate or
>   bittersweet

Grease and lightly flour, or spray with vegetable shortening spray, one 10" x 15" x 1" jelly roll pan.

Cream butter and sugar together with mixer at low speed. Continuing to beat, add chocolate syrup. Add eggs and mix well. Sift together flour and baking powder and blend into batter. Add vanilla, mixing thoroughly. Pour into prepared pan and bake for 20-23 minutes or until cake pulls away from sides of pan. Cool on rack.

To prepare icing, cut butter into small pieces and combine with sugar and cream in a small saucepan. Bring to a boil and boil for two minutes, stirring almost continuously. Remove from heat and add chocolate bits. Beat until icing is smooth and shiny. Spread immediately on cooled cake. (Icing will be thin, but will set up quickly.) Score cake in desired-size squares. Press a pecan half in center of each square, if you wish. Cut into squares and store in tightly covered container in cool place.

Chocolate Chip Cookies

Almost everyone knows that 1929 marked the beginning of the Great Depression. Practically no one seems to know that it was also the year that Ruth Wakefield developed the chocolate chip cookie (or "Toll House Chocolate Crunch Cookies", as the original published version was titled). The name came from the fact that Mrs. Wakefield served the cookies at a charming Inn she and her husband operated in an old Massachusetts Toll House, a place where in times-past passengers had eaten, changed horses and paid tolls. The "chocolate crunch" referred not to chocolate tidbits as we know them today but to the original ingredient "2 - 7-oz. bars of bittersweet chocolate cut in pieces the size of pea". While Mrs. Wakefield included a number of other recipes featured at her Inn in her book, it is unlikely that any of them will ever achieve the fame of the Toll House Chocolate Crunch.

Although I hate to admit it, since I was born in 1929, I can remember when the Toll House cookies my mother made were a novelty and not America's favorite cookie (which the chocolate chip has become). Then there was only one version; now there seem to be hundreds and almost everyone has a favorite. I've included two—one a thin, crispy cookie and the other a softer thicker cookie. Add one or both to your Christmas collection because you absolutely can't go wrong with chocolate chip cookies as a gift.

Chocolate Chip #1

Chocolate Chip #1 . . . a thin, crispy cookie much like the original.

Preheat oven to 350°. Makes 4 dozen.

> 1 1/2 cups all-purpose flour
> 1/2 teaspoon baking soda
> 1/2 teaspoon baking powder
> 1/2 teaspoon salt
> 1 cup butter or margarine
> 1/3 cup granulated sugar
> 1/2 cup brown sugar
> 2 eggs
> 1 teaspoon vanilla extract
> 1 12-ounce package semisweet
>   chocolate bits
> 3/4 cup pecans or walnuts, coarsely
>   broken (optional)

Sift together the first four ingredients and set aside. Cream softened butter or margarine and add sugars (brown and granulated) gradually, continuing to cream. When sugar is completely incorporated, add eggs and vanilla, beating thoroughly. Add flour and mix thoroughly. Stir in chocolate bits and nuts and drop by rounded teaspoonsful onto greased or foil-lined cookie sheets about 2 1/2" apart. Bake 12-15 minutes or until lightly browned. Remove to wire rack to cool thoroughly before storing in airtight container.

Chocolate Chip #2

Chocolate Chip #2 . . . a thicker, softer cookie than the first version! They keep well and travel well, so they're great to include in boxes for those far-away friends and relatives. Also, because this recipe calls for egg yolks only, it's a good recipe to use when you've been making meringues, angel food cakes or other goodies that call only for egg whites.

Preheat oven to 350°. Makes approximately 4½ dozen.

1 3/4 cups all-purpose flour
1 teaspoon baking powder
1/4 teaspoon salt
1 teaspoon baking soda
3/4 cup butter or margarine
1/2 cup brown sugar
1/2 cup granulated sugar
6 egg yolks
1 tablespoon sour cream
1 teaspoon vanilla
1 12-ounce package chocolate semisweet bits
1 cup coarsely broken nuts—pecans or walnuts

Sift together first four ingredients, and set aside. Cream together softened butter or margarine and sugars until they are light and fluffy. Add egg yolks, vanilla and sour cream and mix thoroughly. Blend in flour until it is completely mixed. Stir in chocolate bits and nuts and drop from tablespoon onto greased or foil-lined cookie sheets. Bake 10-12 minutes until lightly browned. Cool on rack before storing in tightly covered container.

Chocolate Madeleines

Purists may think Madeleine pans should be saved for the classic version of this treat only. I disagree. These chocolate ones are light and delicious, and mixed on a platter or packed in a tin with the classic Madeleines, they provide an interesting contrast of color and taste. A light dusting of confectioner's sugar adds a bit of extra sweetness and looks pretty, too.

Preheat oven to 350°. Makes 24.

1/2 cup butter, softened
1/2 cup granulated sugar, sifted
1 egg, at room temperature
3/8 cup all-purpose flour
3/4 teaspoon baking powder
1/8 teaspoon salt
3/8 cup unsweetened cocoa
2 tablespoons Cointreau or other
    orange liqueur
1 egg white

Grease madeleine pans or spray with vegetable oil spray. Cream butter and add sugar gradually, continuing to cream until well blended. Add egg and beat well. Sift together flour, baking powder, salt and cocoa. Add to batter with the liqueur and beat at medium speed until well mixed. In a separate bowl beat the one egg white until it stands in stiff peaks. Fold into chocolate batter and blend completely. Fill madeleine pans, using approximately one rounded teaspoonful of batter in each space. Bake 12-15 minutes. Cool on rack partially. Then remove from pan; turn flat side down, and dust with confectioner's sugar. When completely cool, store in a tightly covered container, in layers separated by wax paper. These may also be packed this way, wrapped securely and frozen for as much as a month, so you can make them before the real holiday rush begins.

Chocolate Pretzels

Besides being one of my very favorite "munching" cookies, this is a fun cookie to make and serve, but especially to give away. A tin packed with a combination of the dark chocolate and the light almond "pretzels" (see recipe on page 31) makes an unusual gift that's sure to be appreciated. The cookies keep beautifully for 2-3 weeks in a tightly covered container, getting crunchier all the time. And since they definitely do not fall in the "quick to make" category, plan to make them before you feel too rushed by holiday pressure to enjoy forming the dough into neat little pretzel shapes.

Preheat oven to 350°. Makes approximately 50.

1 3/4 cups all-purpose flour
1/2 cup unsweetened cocoa
1 teaspoon baking powder
1/8 teaspoon salt
1/2 cup butter or margarine
3/4 cup sugar
1 tablespoon rum, preferably dark
2 eggs
1 teaspoon water
1/2 cup coarse sugar (pearl sugar,
    decorating sugar or crushed sugar cubes)

Sift together the first four ingredients and set aside. Cream butter and sugar together. Add one egg and rum and beat well. Add flour/cocoa and mix thoroughly. Chill dough for several hours.

When ready to bake, grease and lightly flour cookie sheets. (When I'm in a hurry, I find the spray preparation containing vegetable shortening and flour works well.) Beat together the remaining egg and the water in a small bowl and set aside.

Working with about one-fourth of the dough at a time, leaving the rest refrigerated, pinch off enough to make a ball about 1" in diameter. On a floured surface, roll this into a rope 8" long* and about the diameter of a thin pencil (3/8"). You can either form the pretzel on the floured surface and transfer it to the cookie sheet with a spatula or you can place your "rope" on the cookie sheet and form the pretzel there. (I find the latter method easier.) To form the pretzel, curve the rope in the center to form a horseshoe shape; then curve the ends around to touch the sides and complete the pretzel. Place cookies about 1" apart on cookie sheet. Brush tops with beaten egg and sprinkle with coarse sugar. Bake 15-18 minutes. Cool on a rack and store in tightly covered container.

*There is certainly no hard and fast law about the 8" length. This just seems to make a nice size cookie. A small ruler or stiff piece of cardboard cut to the length you prefer will help you to make the cookies uniform in size which will not affect their taste at all, but will look very professional.

You may prefer nice straight pretzels to the fancy shapes, in which case simply roll a small piece of dough between your palms or on a floured surface to the desired size. Brush with egg, sprinkle with sugar and enjoy chocolate stick pretzels.

43

Date Bars

A delightfully easy to make, "chewy" bar cookie that's nice to include in an assortment . . . but really better packed all by themselves to make a tin full of rich goodness. These, too, can be baked early, as they soften and become better after several days stored in a tightly covered container.

Preheat oven to 325°. Makes 48 bars, approximately 1"x2".

1 1/3 cups granulated sugar
1 1/2 cups all-purpose flour
1 teaspoon baking powder
1 teaspoon salt
2 eggs
2 tablespoons sour cream
1 cup chopped English walnuts
1 8-ounce package chopped dates
1 teaspoon vanilla

Grease a 9"x13"x2" pan. Sift together the sugar, flour, baking powder and salt. In a measuring cup, beat the two eggs and stir in the sour cream, whisking together until well blended. Then stir into dry mixture. Add nuts, dates and vanilla, stirring until well mixed. Batter will be rather stiff. Spoon into pan and bake 30 minutes. Allow to partially cool on rack before cutting into bars and removing from pan. When completely cool, store in tightly covered container.

Filled Lemon Drops

Husbands are a great help in compiling a cookbook. They taste, often criticize, occasionally praise (those are the gold-star recipes), and offer often unsolicited but usually helpful advice. In testing recipes for this book, I tended to work in categories—sugar cookies one week, chocolate cookies the next, etc. During a sugar cookie session, my husband asked rather plaintively if I did not have any flavoring except vanilla. "I just made some lemon ones," I answered, pointing them out.

44

"Well," he said after a couple of bites, *"they aren't very* lemony", *and went back to his television program. I tasted again and he was right. They weren't very lemony. After a few mouth-puckering experiments that were too lemony, I produced this cookie which got an "O.K." from husband Clay and is hereby included for other lemon-lovers. As a bonus, the cookies look pretty, pack easily and keep well.*

Preheat oven to 400°. Makes 16 double cookies

> 1 1/8 cups all-purpose flour
> 1/8 teaspoon salt
> 1/2 cup margarine or butter
> 3/8 cup confectioner's sugar
> 1 1/2 teaspoons lemon extract
> 1/2 teaspoon yellow food coloring (optional)

Lemon filling recipe follows.

Sift together flour and salt and set aside. Mix together margarine or butter, confectioner's sugar and lemon extract, creaming thoroughly. Stir in flour and food coloring, if used, and mix well. Wrap in transparent wrap or place in tightly covered container and chill for at least one hour. Pinch off small pieces of dough and roll between palms to form balls about 1/2" to 3/4" in diameter. Flatten slightly and place on ungreased cookie sheet about 1 1/2" apart. Bake 8-10 minutes until edges are very slightly browned. Cool on rack. When cool enough to handle, put together with lemon filling and roll in confectioner's sugar. Store in tightly covered container.

LEMON FILLING

> 1/4 cup granulated sugar
> 2 1/4 teaspoons cornstarch
> 1/8 teaspoon salt
> 1/4 cup water
> 1 tablespoon butter or margarine
> 1 teaspoon grated lemon rind
> 1 1/2 tablespoons lemon juice
> 2 drops yellow food coloring (optional)

Mix sugar, cornstarch and salt in small heavy saucepan. Stir in other ingredients and cook over medium heat, stirring often, until mixture thickens and comes to a boil. Boil for one minute, stirring constantly. Remove from heat and cool.

Giant Malteds

These cookies were "born" a lot of years ago out of desperation. I was just out of college and teaching a large Sunday School class of six-year olds. I couldn't afford to buy presents for all of them and the thought of baking enough cookies to pack a box for each child was overwhelming. My sister Edythe, who always seemed to be able to solve my problems, came up with the idea for these easy-to-make cookies that would be unusual enough to charm the children and large enough so that we'd need to make only one per child. They were (pardon the pun) a "giant" success.

You'll find they appeal to adults as much as to children, so bake a lot! I sometimes fill a basket of individually wrapped cookies, tie a Christmas ribbon on the handle and place it near my door for a supply of small gifts for unexpected guests. The cookies also make fun take-home favors for holiday party guests. (Try decorating some with "happy faces" for birthday parties any time of the year.) One of the nicest ways to use them, however, is to fill a basket with individually wrapped cookies and take them to a near-by nursing home or children's hospital ward for distribution to all whose diets allow sweets. You—and your giant cookies—will be long remembered.

Preheat oven to 375°. Makes 18 cookies.

1 cup butter or margarine, softened
2 cups firmly packed light brown sugar
2 eggs
4 cups all-purpose flour
2 teaspoons baking powder
1/2 teaspoon baking soda
1/2 teaspooon salt
1 cup chocolate malted milk powder
1/3 cup sour cream
1 1/2 teaspoons vanilla

Icing recipe follows.

46

Combine butter and sugar, creaming thoroughly. Using mixer at medium speed, add two unbeaten eggs. Sift together flour, baking powder, baking soda and salt. Gradually add about half the flour and half the malted milk powder to batter, mixing well. Blend in sour cream and vanilla. Add remaining dry ingredients, mixing thoroughly. Chill for 3-4 hours. Using about one-third of the dough at a time, roll out on floured surface and cut with 1-pound coffee can. Transfer to lightly greased cookie sheet and bake 10-12 minutes. Allow to cool completely on rack before icing.

ICING

1/4 cup butter
1/2 cup chocolate malted milk powder
1/4 cup milk
1 teaspoon vanilla
2-2 1/4 cups confectioner's sugar
Nuts, chocolate sprinkles, or candied
    cherries for decoration

Combine first three ingredients and cook over low heat, stirring constantly, until mixture thickens. Remove from heat and add vanilla. Add confectioner's sugar, beating until icing is smooth and has a good spreading consistency. Ice cooled cookies and decorate with pecan or almond halves, chocolate sprinkles or candied red and green cherries. Store in tightly covered container.

Lacy Roll-Ups

This is an elegant looking and delicious cookie that inevitably seems to impress people with your baking skill. When I was small and watched my mother make these, working quickly to roll the cookies into neat cylinders, I thought it was something I could never learn to do. When I did try it, I found it easier than I thought, though mine didn't look quite like mother's. They did, though, after a little practice and I've always loved serving them. I think you will, too, so do try them.

Preheat oven to 375°. Makes 12.

1/4 cup finely ground blanched almonds
1/4 cup granulated sugar
1/4 cup butter
1 tablespoon flour
1 tablespoon milk

Lightly grease and flour cookie sheet. Combine all ingredients in small heavy saucepan over medium heat, stirring constantly until butter is melted and mixture is smooth.

For each cookie, drop a heaping teaspoonful of batter onto prepared cookie sheet, putting only 4 or 5 cookies on one sheet. Bake 5 minutes. (Cookies will be very thin and lacy.) Remove and cool on rack for 2-3 minutes. Working quickly, loosen cookies with a wide spatula and flip over onto a wax paper covered flat surface. Roll quickly around the handle of a wooden spoon and slide the cookie "cylinder" off the handle, seam side down, and allow to cool completely. If cookies become too brittle to roll, put back in the oven for several seconds to soften.

When completely cool, serve as they are or fill with the following. If not using immediately, store cookies in tightly covered container and fill only when ready to use.

BRANDY CREAM
1/4 cup butter
2/3 cup sifted confectioner's sugar
2 teaspoons brandy

Beat all ingredients together until smooth and creamy. Put in pastry tube fitted with small tip and pipe into one end of pastry cylinder; turn cylinder and pipe cream into the other end. Refrigerate until ready to serve.

Lemon Squares

My good-cook sister-in-law Carrie, who gave me this recipe, recently welcomed me home from a lengthy stay in the hospital with a plate of these, and after the bland taste of hospital food, nothing ever tasted quite so good. They also make easy "welcome to the neighborhood" gifts anytime of the year. And they're marvelous take-along sweets for summer picnics or fall football game tailgate lunches.

But their tart, fresh taste seems especially welcome during the holidays amid all the chocolate, nut and spice flavored goodies. In addition to being a delicious snack, they make a perfect light dessert for busy-day meals. So pack tins with them and surprise good friends or neighbors early in the season.

Another "plus" for the recipe is the fact that it can be doubled and still turn out perfectly.

Preheat oven to 350°. Makes 16 to 20 2" squares.

CRUST

1/4 cup butter or margarine
1/4 cup confectioner's sugar
1 cup flour, unsifted
1/8 teaspoon salt

TOPPING

2 eggs
1 cup sugar
2 tablespoons flour, sifted
1/2 tsp. baking powder
3 tablespoons lemon juice
1 tablespoon grated lemon rind (optional)
Confectioner's sugar (optional)

Grease 9" square pan or 8" x 10" rectangular pan and set aside.

To make crust, cream butter thoroughly. Add sugar, flour and salt, continuing to cream until completely mixed. (This will be dry and crumbly.) Spread over bottom of pan and press down with hand firmly and evenly to form crust. Bake 15 minutes. Remove from oven and allow to cool.

Meanwhile, beat eggs slightly and mix in by hand (do not use mixer) sugar, lemon juice and lemon rind. Fold in flour and baking powder and pour over cooled crust. Bake 20 minutes. Cool on rack and dust with confectioner's sugar, if you wish, before cutting into squares.

Madeleines

Long before we knew anything about Marcel Proust who, according to most cookbook authors, immortalized Madeleines as "plump little cakes", we loved it when mother baked what we called her "seashell" cookies and let us have them still warm from the oven. Whether my widely read mother was fond of Proust or not, I don't know. But I do know she treasured her heavy Madeleine pans and passed them along to me. If you weren't lucky enough to inherit pans, you'll find them a good investment because the small cakes are perfect to serve with anything from cold champagne to hot chocolate or milk.

These keep up to a week, tightly covered, and freeze beautifully, so you can get a head start on Christmas by baking a supply early in the season for later serving or gift-giving.

A dusting of confectioner's sugar on the top at the last moment adds a festive touch and an extra bit of sweetness.

Another way to serve them was suggested to me by an English friend who said her family always had them for tea brushed with warmed currant jelly and sprinkled with grated or flaked coconut. Absolutely addictive!

Preheat oven to 400°. Makes 2 dozen*.

1/4 cup butter, melted and cooled
2 eggs
1/8 teaspoon salt
1/3 cup sugar
1/2 teaspoon vanilla
1/2 cup cake flour
1/2 teaspoon mace
Confectioner's Sugar (optional) or
1/4 cup currant jelly, warmed (optional)
1/2 cup flaked or grated coconut (optional)

Grease and flour two Madeleine pans and set aside. (*If you have only one pan, divide the recipe in half because these really are better if they are baked immediately after mixing.)

Melt butter and set aside to cool. Sift sugar and set aside. Sift together flour and mace and set aside. Beat eggs and salt until frothy. Add sugar slowly and continue beating until batter is almost the consistency of whipped cream. (about 5 minutes with electric mixer). Beat in vanilla and mace. Add flour slowly, blending in. Finally, blend in melted butter and pour into Madeleine molds immediately filling each about 3/4 full. Bake 10-12 minutes and cool on rack slightly before removing from pans. (It may be necessary to loosen the edges carefully with a small sharp-pointed knife.)

If freezing, arrange in layers, separated by wax paper, in airtight container and freeze immediately. Add any optional toppings after thawing, when ready to serve.

If serving immediately, dust tops of Madeleines with confectioner's sugar. Or brush tops with warmed currant jelly and sprinkle with coconut.

Meringue Clouds

An incredibly easy cookie, but time-consuming because the baking time is longer than average. Light as air (and excellent for the dieters on your list), they can be left white or tinted any desired color.

Preheat oven to 300°.

2 egg whites
1/8 teaspoon salt
2/3 cup granulated sugar, sifted
1/2 teaspoon almond extract*
1/2 cup finely ground almonds*
3-4 drops of food coloring (optional)
*maple flavoring and pecans or vanilla flavoring and walnuts may be substituted if you prefer.

Beat egg whites and salt until foamy. Add sugar very gradually, continuing to beat at high speed. Add extract and beat until sugar is completely dissolved (4-5 minutes) and mixture stands in stiff peaks. Fold in nuts and food coloring if used. Drop by teaspoonsful on foil-lined cookie sheets. Bake 30 minutes. Remove from oven and slide foil sheets onto rack. When cookies are completely cool, carefully peel from foil and store in airtight containers.

Southern Pecan Squares

When I was young, I loved my mother's pecan pie, but hated the "fuss" of pie baking. Since I loved making cookies, I thought I must be able to achieve some of the same taste in a bar cookie and my experimentation led to this result. Relatively easy, it keeps well, is popular, and like most bar cookies, packs well.

Preheat oven to 350°. Makes approximately 24 squares.

CRUST
3/4 cup butter or margarine, melted and cooled
2 cups flour
1 cup finely chopped pecans

TOPPING
3 eggs
2/3 cups sugar
1 cup dark corn syrup
1/3 cup butter or margarine melted
1/4 teaspoon salt
1 cup coarsely ground or chopped pecans

Very lightly grease and flour 9" x 13" baking dish or pan, or spray with vegetable oil spray.

Stir together all ingredients for the crust and press evenly into bottom of pan. Bake 15-20 minutes. Remove and cool on rack.

In the meantime, prepare the topping. Thoroughly beat egg until light in color. Add sugar and continue to beat, add syrup, melted butter and 3/4 cup nuts. Pour over cooled crust and sprinkle remaining 1/4 cup nuts on top. Bake an additional 20-25 minutes or until a cake tester comes out clean. Remove to rack and cool completely. Cut in squares, approximately 2" x 2".

Pack in layers, separated by wax paper, in tightly covered container and store in cool place.

Decorated Sugar Cookies

The first decorated Christmas sugar cookies I remember were given to me when I was very small by an elderly German friend of my mother. They were small rabbits and chickens, very thin and a bit spicy, iced in white and sprinkled with pastel candies. I was enchanted by them and when one finally broke, I was torn between tears at losing it and delight at being able to eat the pieces.

The next Christmas she gave me two cutters along with the cookies, and that was the beginning of my life-long love affair with cookies and with cookie cutters. My collection is now large and varied, but each year with my angels, Santas and other intricate holiday shapes, I bake a few bunnies and chicks in fond remembrance of the kindly and portly "Mrs. Bea" who never knew how much joy she really gave me.

Through the years I was never able to develop a dough that would roll thinly and have a taste that matched a childhood memory. So, I settled for the following sugar cookie recipe which works well and continues to delight both my young and old friends.

They keep, packed in a tightly covered container, practically forever, so bake them early. The decorating is a labor of love and needs to be enjoyed at leisure before the most hectic holiday rush begins.

Preheat oven to 375°. Makes 24-36 cookies, depending upon size.

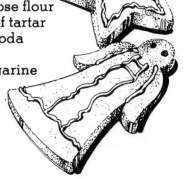

3 1/2 cups all-purpose flour
2 teaspoons cream of tartar
1 teaspoon baking soda
1/2 teaspoon salt
1 cup butter or margarine
1 1/2 cups sugar
3 eggs
1 teaspoon vanilla

Sift together the first four ingredients and set aside. Cream together the butter and sugar until light and fluffy. Add eggs, one at a time, mixing well after each addition. Add vanilla and mix well. Add flour mixture gradually to batter, mixing thoroughly. Chill 4-5 hours. Working with only about one-fourth of the dough at a time (leaving the remainder in the refrigerator), roll on floured surface to 1/8"-1/4" thickness. Cut into desired shapes and transfer to ungreased cookie sheet, placing about 1" apart. (If they are very thin, you may find a spatula helpful in placing the cookies on the baking sheet.) If you wish to hang them on your Christmas tree, make a small hole in the top of each cookie with a toothpick. Bake 5-8 minutes (smaller shapes take less time, so watch carefully so they do not become too brown—only the edges should be lightly browned). Cool on rack and allow to cool completely before decorating.

Cookies may be frosted with any plain frosting and trimmed with pastel candy "sprinkles", nuts or anything else you like. Or you may "paint" on more intricate designs with the following icing.

DECORATOR ICING
2 cups confectioner's sugar
1-2 tablespoons water
Food coloring

Mix together sugar and 1 tablespoon of water in small mixing bowl. Add water, a little at a time, mixing until icing is of spreading consistency. Divide into as many portions in small bowls or saucers as the number of colors you wish to use. Then add food coloring to each portion of icing. This can be applied to cookies with a decorator's tube, but I find it easier and more effective to use a small paint brush and "paint" the icing on.

Easy Sugar Cookies

*I call these my "everyday" sugar cookies because they are
so easy to make, but they're crisp enough and good enough to
delight anyone and with the addition of a sprinkle of colored
sugar, they make a pretty addition to any Christmas gift box.*

Preheat oven to 350°. Makes 3 dozen.

> **3/4 cup butter or margarine, softened**
> **3/4 cup granulated sugar**
> **2 1/3 cups all-purpose flour**
> **1/4 teaspoon salt**
> **1 1/2 teaspoons baking powder**
> **1 tablespoon milk**
> **1 egg**
> **2 teaspoons finely grated lemon peel**

Cream butter thoroughly and gradually add sugar, continuing to beat until completely blended. Sift together flour,
salt and baking powder and set aside. Beat egg and milk
together until completely blended. Add flour, alternately with
egg/milk mixture, to batter, continuing to beat until thoroughly mixed. Mix in lemon peel. Chill dough for several
hours. Working with about one-fourth of the dough at a time,
leaving the rest refrigerated, roll into small balls about 1" in
diameter. Place 2" apart on lightly greased or foil-lined cookie
sheet. With fork dipped in flour, flatten balls, first one way and
then the other to make a criss-cross pattern. Sprinkle with
granulated sugar, plain or colored, and bake for 12-15 minutes. Remove to rack to cool. If you wish, sprinkle with additional sugar while still warm. When completely cool, pack in
tightly covered container.

Sugar Cream Crispies

When I was growing up, we called these "tea biscuits" because we always served them at teas. And about the time I was in high school and college, afternoon teas were very popular in my small southern town. We had getting-out-of-school teas, back-to-school teas, and as we grew a bit older, engagement and bridal teas, and even baby-shower teas. These crispy little cookies were almost always included because by varying the design of the cookie cutter and the color of the sugar we dipped the cookies in, we could make them fit any occasion and any color scheme. In recent years, however, they've become a stand-by in my Christmas collection because I can get beautiful stars and trees and bells and hearts that are easier to make and better to eat than the traditional decorated sugar cookie. They'll keep for up to two weeks in an airtight container, but pack them carefully for they are fragile.

Preheat oven to 375°. Makes 5 dozen.

> 1 cup margarine or butter softened
> 2 cups all-purpose flour
> 1/3 cup whipping cream
> granulated sugar

Cream softened butter or margarine. Add flour and cream and mix well. Wrap in transparent wrap or put in a tightly covered container and chill for several hours. When ready to bake, remove only about one-fourth of the dough from the refrigerator at a time. Roll between two pieces of lightly floured waxed paper and cut in small rounds or decorative shapes. Put about a cup of granulated sugar in a flat bowl and drop cookies in this, turning them over until they are completely coated with sugar before placing them on ungreased cookie sheet. (Colored granulated sugar may be used.) Prick each cookie two or three times with a fork and bake 8-10 minutes. Cool on rack and store in tightly covered container.

Thumbprints

As a child, this was one of my very favorite cookies—both because it was good and because it was fun to help make. Not only would mother let me help roll the dough into balls and then in a coating of nuts, she'd let me poke my finger in the top of each ball (which really seemed like something I shouldn't be allowed to do—so naturally I enjoyed it). Thumbprints are still among my favorite cookies because they're buttery and good and pretty, and can be made early and frozen.

Preheat oven to 350° when ready to bake cookies. Makes 48.

> 1 cup butter or margarine, softened
> 1/2 cup granulated sugar
> 2 egg yolks
> 1 teaspoon vanilla extract
> 2 cups all-purpose flour
> 1/2 teaspoon salt
> 1/2 cup finely ground pecans
> 6 ounces currant jelly (or flavor of your choice)

Cream butter and sugar together until light and fluffy. Add egg yolks and vanilla and continue beating until well mixed. Sift flour and salt together and add gradually, mixing until well blended. Refrigerate dough for at least one hour.

When ready to make cookies, preheat oven to 350°. Take out about one-fourth of the dough, leaving the rest refrigerated. Pinch off small pieces and roll in balls, about 3/4" to 1" in diameter. Roll in finely ground nuts and place on ungreased baking sheets about 2" apart. Using your thumb (or the end of a wooden spoon), make an indentation in the top of each cookie. Bake 10 minutes and remove from oven. While cookies are hot, make the indentation again(This time, it may be best to use the end of a wooden spoon rather than fingers to avoid the possibility of a burn.) and fill each "hole" with currant jelly (about 1/4 teaspoon). Bake 5 more minutes. Remove from oven and cool on rack. Repeat until all cookies are baked. Store in tightly covered container in cool place.

Please note that these freeze well, so if you want to make them early (as much as several weeks), allow them to cool completely, arrange in layers, separated by wax paper, and put in freezer container or wrap securely in foil. Label, date, and relax until gift giving time rolls around.

Wedding Cookies

Despite the name (which I use because it was handed down to me with recipe), these are really ideal Christmas cookies for several reasons. They're pretty (look like miniature snowballs); they're incredibly easy and fast to make; they're melt-in-the-mouth delicious and appeal to almost everyone; and best of all, they positively never fail. Once you try these, you're sure to add them to your collection of "tried and true" recipes.

Preheat oven to 350°. Makes approximately 7 dozen.

> 1 cup butter, softened
> 2 cups flour (measured before sifting)
> 1 cup pecans or other nuts, chopped very fine
> 2 teaspoons vanilla
> Confectioner's sugar

Sift flour. Combine butter and flour, using a wooden spoon or your hands, until thoroughly mixed. Stir in nuts and vanilla. Mixture will be quite stiff. Roll bits of dough between the palms of your hands to form balls approximately the diameter of a nickel. Place about 1 1/2" apart and bake 12-15 minutes until lightly browned. Cool on rack. When cookies are barely warm to the touch, roll in confectioner's sugar and allow to "rest" for a few minutes before packing into tins.

White Brownies

During World War II, my older brother and many friends were scattered across the world in various branches of the armed forces. So my mother, my sister and I joined other women "on the home front" in baking as many sweets as sugar rationing would allow to send to our fighting men. Because they packed well, kept for a long time and were popular, brownies were included in almost every box. So many brownies in fact that we often vowed never to bake another.

Some years later, however, I discovered "white chocolate" and fell in love with its mild flavor. Looking for ways to use it, I pulled out the old brownie recipe and started experimenting. The result was a pleasantly different white brownie. While some of mine still go in "care" packages to hungry young servicemen and collegians year 'round, my favorite time to bake them is the holiday season. They make marvelous gifts, packed in tins, or baked in disposable foil pans, wrapped in clear wrap and tied with bright Christmas ribbons.

Preheat oven to 325°. Makes approximately 54 2" squares.

- 7 ounces white chocolate
- 3/4 cup butter or margarine
- 6 eggs
- 3 cups granulated sugar
- 1 1/2 teaspoons almond flavoring
- 1 1/2 cups all-purpose flour
- 1/2 teaspoon salt
- 1 1/2 cups walnuts or pecans, chopped

Grease and flour a 12"x 18" baking pan or 2-9"x 12" pans.

Melt chocolate in top of double boiler over hot (not boiling) water. Set aside to cool. Melt butter and set aside to cool.

Beat eggs and sugar together until light in color. Blend in flavoring, butter and chocolate. Sift together flour and salt. Add flour, together with nuts to batter, blending, using low speed on mixer until thoroughly mixed. Pour in prepared pan and bake for 20-25 minutes until top appears dry and slightly crusty. Cool completely on rack before cutting.

Whoopie Pies

My friends say that when I travel, I bring back recipes instead of souvenirs. But those recipes are my souvenirs. My husband and I re-live many marvelous trips and experiences as we eat or drink something at home that we've shared together in far-away Mexico or Hawaii or a nearby mountain Inn. Recently, we spent a long weekend in the Amish country in Pennsylvania where I met interesting people, saw beautiful countryside and ate marvelous food. I had heard of Shoo Fly Pie and Funnel Cake (both regional favorites), but when the young desk clerk at the hotel asked if I'd eaten Whoopie Pies, I thought he must be kidding. He wasn't. The next day I saw and sampled Whoopie Pies in a fantastic farmer's market where the assortment of homemade sausages, cheeses, pastries and other goodies delighted all my senses. After talking to local cooks, I came home with a variety of Whoopie Pie directions, and after a little experimentation, arrived at this recipe. This is no dainty tea-time cookie, but a hearty snack just asking for a cold glass of milk. While you may not want to include them in some of your gift collections of cookies, try packing a tin of these soft chocolate "sandwiches", individually wrapped, for a friend with children or a chocolate-loving husband. They freeze well for up to a month, and keep well in a tightly covered container, for at least a week. And they make popular lunchbox desserts for the "brown bag" crowd.

Preheat oven to 400°. Makes 18 "sandwiches".

> 1/2 cup **vegetable shortening**
> 1 cup granulated sugar
> 1 egg
> 1 teaspoon vanilla
> 2 cups sifted all-purpose flour
> 1 teaspoon salt
> 1/2 cup unsweetened cocoa
> 1/2 cup sour milk (or 1/4 cup sour cream
>   blended with 1/2 cup milk)
> 1/2 cup hot water
> 1 teaspoon soda

Cream shortening and sugar together. Add egg and vanilla and beat well. Sift together flour, salt, and cocoa and add to batter alternately with milk. Stir baking soda into hot water and add to batter, continuing to beat until thoroughly mixed and batter is smooth. Drop from a teaspoon onto lightly greased cookie sheet, about 2 1/2" apart. (A heaping teaspoon of batter will give you about a 3" diameter cookie. If you wish smaller cookies, use a proportionately smaller amount—perhaps a level teaspoon of batter). Bake 6-8 minutes and cool on rack. Remove from cookie sheet with wide spatula and put two cookies, flat sides facing, together with the following filling. After filling, store in layers, separated by wax paper in tightly covered container in cool place. Or wrap each "sandwich" individually in plastic wrap and store in tightly covered container. These may be frozen, after being securely wrapped, for up to 1 month.

FILLING
1/2 cup vegetable shortening
2 1/4 cups powdered sugar
1 egg white
1/8 teaspoon salt
1 teaspoon vanilla (or if you prefer a hint of
    almond, use 1/2 teaspoon vanilla and
    1/2 teaspoon almond flavoring)

Blend all ingredients together with mixer at low speed and then beat until smooth and creamy.

Notes on Candy Making

The candy recipes that follow are intended primarily for the novice, for those people who just want to make a few batches of candy for the family or to use for holiday gifts.

They are, for the most part, virtually "fail-safe" so that your candy-making can be fun, can be a family project, and can add to, rather than detract from, your holiday enjoyment.

If you find yourself loving every minute and getting results you're proud of, you may well want to pursue the subject with specialized books on candy making or perhaps by taking one of the many short courses offered in almost every locality now. There is a real revival of interest in candy making, and you may find yourself with a brand new cooking interest. I hope that you do.

For the moment, however, and for the recipes that follow, there are a few "tools" that are essential to your success. They include a good candy thermometer, a double boiler, a small deep heavy saucepan, wooden spoons and a wire whisk; and a portable electric mixer is most helpful.

Before starting, be sure that you have plenty of aluminum foil and wax paper on hand as well as cookie sheets or flat platters. And clear your kitchen counters to give yourself as much working space as possible. Also, it's a good idea to check the recipes you want to try and be sure that you have all the necessary ingredients on hand before you start. (Candy making does not lend itself to stopping in the middle of a batch to run to the store to pick up a forgotten item.)

As in cookie-making, approach your candy making project with the intention of enjoying it. You will. If you have a husband who volunteers to help or children who want to take part, let them. If the end results aren't perfect, you'll still end up with something that tastes good . . . one of the nicest rewards of candy making.

So make this a "sweet" holiday at your house with home-made candy. You'll be so proud of your accomplishments.

Chocolate Dipping

There are several ways to go about chocolate dipping (and several different combinations of ingredients that can be used), and the method you use will depend a great deal on what ingredients are readily available to you, how much experience you have and, simply, what your personal preference is.

Regardless of the method you choose, there are several rules that must be followed to insure success.

Chocolate dipping is best done in a moderately heated room with low humidity, free of steam, and with no direct drafts in the area where you're actually dipping the chocolates.

Chocolate must always be melted slowly. The water in the bottom of the double boiler should be hot, not boiling or steaming, and it should not touch the bottom of the pan in which the chocolate is melting.

Chocolate should be grated or broken into small pieces before melting and should be stirred occasionally with a spatula or wooden spoon to insure even melting.

Chocolate should always be allowed to cool slowly.

Having outlined the general ground rules for dipping chocolates, it's time to consider the materials to be used.

Chocolate Bits and Paraffin

The first candy dipped in chocolate I ever made, I used for the dipping mixture, bittersweet chocolate baking bits and slivered paraffin wax melted together. This method, while far from professional, is still used by many home candy makers simply because these ingredients are readily available in supermarkets in all areas of the country. And as long as the amount of wax used is not excessive, the taste of the finished product is acceptable. A good rule of thumb is to use about 1/6 of a block of paraffin wax, shaved, with 12 ounces of chocolate bits. This will coat about 50 small (approximately 3/4") candy centers. However, since it is better to work with at least a pound to a pound and a half of chocolate when dipping, try using two 12-ounce packages of chocolate and 1/3 block paraffin wax (approximately 1 ounce) melted in the top of a double boiler. When the chocolate has melted and is smooth, remove from heat and stir until it cools to a point where a bit dropped on wax paper will harden in about 90 seconds. (Leftover chocolate can be saved and reheated for use at a later candy-making session, or used up at once by dipping pecan or walnut halves ... or fruit sections for "instant" family treats. (Dipped fruit really should be eaten the same day.)

Summer Coating

If there is a candy or confectioner's supply store in your area, summer coating (often called "white chocolate") will be available to you. It is usually available in a variety of colors and flavors and its use simplifies the dipping process immeasurably. Simply break the chocolate into small pieces and place in the top of a double boiler, keeping earlier rules in mind. Melt, stirring occasionally, until chocolate reaches a temperature of 125°. Remove from heat and allow the coating to cool to 105°, at which point it is ready to use. Should it become too cool to work easily, repeat the heating and cooling process and continue dipping. This chocolate is delicious eaten "as is" and there are a number of suggestions on page 73 for using any that may be left over from dipping.

Blended Coating

This consists of a combination of unsweetened pure chocolate used for baking (read the label and be sure that it is pure, natural chocolate) which can be readily purchased in 8-ounce packages in most local stores, and the summer coating described above. (Note: 4 ounces of chocolate will give you approximately 1 cup of grated chocolate). Depending upon the flavor you want, vary the combination of the two ingredients. 2 cups of broken or grated summer coating and 2 cups of grated unsweetened chocolate will give you a rich, rather sweet dark chocolate. A mixture of 1 cup of the summer coating and 3 cups of the grated unsweetened chocolate will give you a bittersweet flavor.

When using this combination, first break the summer coating into small pieces and melt, following direction given earlier. Remove from heat and stir in the grated unsweetened chocolate about a tablespoonful at a time until the mixture is completely blended and cooled until about "pudding" consistency or a temperature of between 90° and 100°. If a small bit dropped on wax paper hardens in about a minute and a half, you're ready to start dipping. If chocolate becomes too cool to work, repeat the heating and cooling process.

Again, don't worry about leftover chocolate. Use some of

the suggestions on page 73 for candy treats that may turn out to be more popular than your original creation.

Tempered Chocolate

The first rule, here, is to buy good quality, pure and natural chocolate. The choice of milk chocolate, dark sweet or bittersweet is a matter of personal preference. However, if the center being dipped is very sweet, the bittersweet chocolate provides a pleasant flavor contrast.

Break the chocolate into small pieces in the top of a double boiler and melt, keeping in mind the general rules outlined earlier. In tempering chocolate, a candy thermometer is an essential, as the chocolate should melt but not reach a temperature above 105° (summer coating mentioned earlier can stand higher temperatures, the reason it is best for summer or warm weather use). At this point, remove from heat and replace the hot water in the bottom of the double boiler with water between 60° and 70°. Allow the chocolate to cool over this water to 80°, continuing to stir. Increase the heat of the water back to 90° and allow the chocolate temperature to go back up to between 80° and 85°. It should now be "tempered" and ready to use. Remember to continue to stir the chocolate occasionally during heating and cooling and during the dipping process.

Dipping Methods

For the actual dipping method, everyone has to perfect his own technique. Professionals are able to drop a center into the warm chocolate, lift it out with two fingers, formed in a "v", scrape the excess chocolate off as they lift it from the pan and form a decorative finish on top almost at the same time. You may want to experiment with this method. Personally, I have always found it necessary to use some "device" to help me and I have found toothpicks most unsatisfactory. You can use a fork, resting the candy on it, dipping it into the chocolate and scraping off the excess against the side of the pan as you lift it out and place it on the wax paper. Or you can improvise by using a piece of wire bent to form a small circle at the end, on which the candy can rest. Or, again, if your area has a candy or confectioner's supply store, you can buy a variety of inexpensive dipping forks which are most helpful.

Almond Bark

This started out to be a way to use up leftover summer coat-ing or "white chocolate" that I was using for dipping candy centers. It proved so popular that I was soon buying "white chocolate" just to make this candy. It is so-o-o good and so-o-o simple. You'll love it.

Preheat oven to 325°.

Makes 4 dozen to 7 dozen pieces (depending upon size and thickness). Use 13"x15" jelly roll pan for candy about 1/4" thick or use 9"x13" baking pan for candy slightly thicker.

2 cups blanched, slivered almonds, toasted
1 1/2 pounds "white chocolate" (or summer
coating)

Spread nuts on cookie sheet and place in preheated oven for 7-10 minutes, stirring occasionally to insure even toasting. Remove from heat and allow to cool slightly while melting chocolate.

Break chocolate into small pieces in top of double boiler and melt over hot—not boiling—water, stirring occasionally to insure even heating and to keep the chocolate smooth. Stir in toasted nuts and spread in foil-lined pan. When the choco-late has partially hardened, you may—if you wish—make lengthwise marks in the surface with the tines of a fork to give a "bark" effect. Allow the chocolate to completely harden before breaking or cutting into desired size pieces. Pack in layers, separated by wax paper, in tightly covered container and store in cool place.

Almond Roca

The nice thing about recipes shared with you by other people is that each time you make the dish, pleasant memories are reawakened. This one was given to me by the daughter of a good friend during a very pleasant party some years ago. The conversation had turned to cooking and I mentioned that I was just really beginning to get into candy-making so Faye insisted that I must try her favorite candy recipe. I did and found why it was a favorite. Try it for some of your favorite people this holiday season.

Makes approximately 7 dozen 1"x 2" bars

> Milk Chocolate Candy Bars (enough to equal
>   9 1/2 ounces)
> 6 ounces finely chopped blanched almonds
> 1 pound butter (do not substitute margarine)
> 2 cups granulated sugar

Sprinkle one-half of the nuts to cover the bottom of a 13" x 15" jelly roll pan. Grate chocolate and sprinkle one-half of it on top of the nuts. In a heavy saucepan, over low heat, cook together butter and sugar, stirring constantly until candy thermometer registers 300°. Pour over chocolate and nuts. Top with remaining chocolate and sprinkle remaining nuts on to make the top layer. Score into desired size bars immediately. Put in refrigerator to harden and then break into pieces as scored.

Bourbon or Brandy Balls

Bourbon Balls are often referred to as a "southern specialty", but I've shared mine with friends from almost every section of the country and most say that a similar sweet is popular where they live.

Our family recipe calls for brandy (which my non-drinking mother kept for medicinal purposes, to age her fruitcakes, and to make this particular holiday treat).

However, bourbon is the important ingredient in recipes friends have shared with me over the years—recipes which fall into several categories: those that have a base of cookie crumbs and those that don't and those that are dipped in chocolate and those that aren't. Whatever you decide to call them, you really should try one—or all—of the versions included here. You can make them early because they keep, tightly covered, exceptionally well (if you hide them); and packed in colorful tins, they make delicious and very special gifts.

Bourbon Balls

This is similar to the brandy balls, but uses bourbon, and vanilla wafer crumbs instead of graham cracker crumbs. It is, perhaps, the most familiar version of this "goodie".

Makes 3 1/2 dozen

> 1 package (12 ounces) vanilla wafers, finely crushed
> 1 cup confectioner's sugar
> 1 cup finely chopped pecans
> 1/4 cup light corn syrup
> 2 tablespoons unsweetened cocoa
> 1/2 cup bourbon
> 1/2 cup granulated sugar

Thoroughly mix all ingredients (using your hands) except the granulated sugar. Pinch off pieces and shape into balls 3/4"-1" in diameter. Roll balls in granulated sugar and store in tightly covered container. Store in cool place. Balls are better after at least three days, but will keep easily up to 3 weeks.

Chocolate-dipped Bourbon Balls

When my good friend Jean announced one day that she was dipping her bourbon balls, I was fascinated, since I'd never made chocolate-covered ones. Since Jean, and husband Troy, (in addition to being very caring, sharing people) are good at everything they do, I knew her bourbon balls had to be good. They were, and I quickly added her recipe to my collection. Since they seemed so unusual to me, I was sur-

prised to receive some as a gift soon after from good neighbors Iris and John. The coincidence is easily explained by the fact that Iris and Jean are sisters-in-law, so I'm not sure whose recipe I have. But regardless of who gets the credit, the candy balls are good and rich, and make gifts that delight any lucky recipient.

Makes 6 dozen 3/4"-1" diameter balls

> 2/3 cup finely chopped pecans
> 1/3 cup bourbon
> 1/4 cup butter or margarine
> 1 pound confectioner's sugar
> 1 1/4 pound chocolate for dipping (see notes on chocolate dipping)

Combine pecans and bourbon in covered dish and allow to soak overnight in refrigerator. Cream together butter and sugar. Add bourbon and nuts. Mix thoroughly and shape into balls 1/2" to 3/4" in diameter. Chill in refrigerator until firm. Coat balls in chocolate by following one of the procedures on pages 63-65.

Brandy Balls

My family recipe still, in many ways, seems the best version of this treat. (But then I'm prejudiced.)

Makes approximately 6 dozen.

> 1 13 1/2 oz. package graham cracker crumbs
> 1 cup confectioner's sugar
> 1/4 cup cocoa
> 8 ounces finely chopped walnuts
> 1/4 cup corn syrup
> 1/3 cup orange liqueur
> 1/3 cup brandy

With your hands, mix all ingredients together until a paste-like dough is formed. Pinch off pieces and roll into balls approximately 3/4"-1" in diameter. Store in tightly covered container in refrigerator overnight. Store in cool place.

Chocolate Bourbon Fudge

In delving into old family recipes, I found that my ancestors, many of whom were "total teetotalers" apparently did not consider the use of alcohol in cooking to be a bad thing, for an incredible number of recipes call for a splash or two of good bourbon whiskey or brandy. In this case, the bourbon seems to give the creamy fudge an added richness while taking away some of the overly sweet taste of many similar candies. It keeps for a long period of time and packs well so it is ideal for gifts that must be mailed long distances.

Makes approximately 5 dozen irresistible pieces

> 2 cups granulated sugar, sifted
> 6 tablespoons unsweetened cocoa
> 3/4 cup cold water
> 1/2 cup butter or margarine
> 1/2 teaspoon almond flavoring
> 2 tablespoons bourbon
> pecan or walnut halves (optional)

Grease sides of a heavy 2 quart saucepan. Combine sugar, cocoa, water and butter. Cook over low heat, stirring constantly until mixture is smooth and sugar is completely dissolved (you should not be able to feel sugar grains when you rub your spoon against the side of the pan). Remove from heat and with a damp sponge, wipe off sugar crystals from sides of the pan). Return to heat and then clip candy thermometer onto pan when liquid starts to boil. Lower heat but keep mixture boiling and cook slowly until thermometer registers 235°F (soft ball stage). Remove from heat and cool to 110°F. Add extract and bourbon and beat with sturdy wooden spoon until mixture thickens and loses its glossy look. (Unless you have a strong right arm and a lot of energy, this is an excellent time to recruit a young friend, or willing husband, to lend a hand.) Drop by scant teaspoonful onto waxed paper and top with nut half if desired. When cooled and set, pack in layers, separated by wax paper. Store in the refrigerator or a cool place, tightly covered.

Chocolate Covered Cherries

For years, I honestly never thought about chocolate covered cherries being available anywhere except in cellophane covered boxes, nor had I ever been especially fond of them.

Then one early December day some years ago, my husband and I stopped by to visit with one of his favorite sisters and found her and her daughter up to their elbows in confectioner's sugar, melted chocolate and bottles of maraschino cherries. There were rows and rows of glossy chocolates lined on kitchen counters and they were both still hard at work. It was absolutely mind-boggling to me. Margaret, my sister-in-law, insisted that we try them, and with polite protestations about having just eaten, we ended up taking a small plastic bag of them home with us. One taste changed any ideas we had from eating "store bought" chocolate-covered cherries. These were a completely different article and they were delicious. As soon as we could get the recipe, we made a batch, bragging on ourselves all afternoon as the candies piled up, and it's been a joint holiday project for us every year since then. They're a lot of work, but they're worth it. A box of these makes an unforgettable gift for the true candy lover, but you'll find that you save them for the most special people on your list.

Packed in tightly covered containers and stored in a cool place, they keep for weeks and weeks, so they can be made as early as November, a real "plus" if your holiday schedule is always hectic.

Makes approximately 120 pieces

- 2 sticks melted butter or margarine
- 1 14-ounce can Eagle brand sweetened condensed milk
- 2-1/2 pounds confectioner's sugar
- 1 teaspoon salt
- 1 3-1/2 ounce can of coconut
- 3 cups pecans or walnuts, ground finely
- 4 8-ounce bottles of maraschino cherries (Look for a brand with the small, not the giant-size cherries. Otherwise, your candies will be too large.)
- 2 pounds of chocolate for dipping (see notes on pages 63-65)

Drain cherries and set aside while preparing fondant. In a heavy saucepan, over low heat, melt the butter and remove from heat and allow to cool slightly. Pour into a large mixing bowl. Add the milk and all other ingredients except cherries and chocolate. Mix with heavy wooden spoon or your hands (I prefer to use my hands) until the fondant is completely mixed, smooth and creamy. It will be very stiff. Form a small ball by rolling a piece between the palms of your hands; flatten slightly and wrap around a cherry, rolling again to form a ball. Place on wax paper covered cookie sheet. Repeat the process until all fondant is used. Put cherries in a cool place while chocolate is being prepared for dipping.

Dip according to directions on pages 63-65 and place in a cool place until completely hardened. Pack in layers, separated by wax paper in tightly covered containers and store in cool place.

Chocolate Nut Clusters

Here's a way to use chocolate left over from dipping centers that may turn out to be a real family favorite! Here again, the proportions are left up to your own judgment and the amount of chocolate you are using.

Melted chocolate (left over from dipping)
Coarsely broken nuts (pecans, walnuts,
**   almonds or peanuts)**

Simply stir nuts into the melted chocolate until you have a good proportion of the two. Then using a teaspoon, drop in small mounds on wax paper lined cookie sheets. Allow to cool and harden completely. Then arrange in layers, separated by wax paper, in tightly covered containers and store in refrigerator or a very cool room until ready to use.

Chocolate Raisin Clusters

Another way to use chocolate left over from dipping centers that may turn out to be so popular, you'll find yourself preparing chocolate just for these. You'll need:

Melted chocolate (left over from dipping)
Seedless Raisins

Here, you'll have to estimate the number of raisins by the amount of chocolate you're using. Stir in enough, so that you have just a sufficient amount of chocolate to bind the raisins together (or fewer if you like chocolate better than raisins). Using a teaspoon, drop small mounds on wax paper lined cookie sheets and allow to cool and harden completely. Pack in tightly covered containers in layers, separated by wax paper and store in refrigerator or in a very cool room.

Cream Cheese Mints

The temptation is to call these mints "easy to make" and I have a sister-in-law who insists they are, as she turns them out by the hundreds, using them for gifts and sharing them freely with family and friends for holiday parties. I concede they are "easy" in that they are practically "no fail", but there is a lot of work involved in mixing and molding the mints. They are so good and so pretty, however, that they are worth the time and effort.

Makes approximately 100 small mints

> 1 4-ounce package cream cheese at
>   room temperature
> 1 pound confectioner's sugar
> 12 drops peppermint oil
> food coloring as desired

Mix softened cream cheese and confectioner's sugar together (I find it easier to use my hands) until a smooth pliant "fondant" is formed. Mix in peppermint oil and if you wish to make more than one color mint, divide into several portions and add a different color to each.

Mints can be molded in small decorative shaped rubber molds (available at candy and confectioner's supply stores and many specialty shops) or you can form the fondant into rolls, chill, and then slice into small rounds. Another possibility is to roll the fondant, between two pieces of wax paper and cut into decorative shapes with small canape or aspic cutters. Store mints in layers, separated by wax paper, in tightly covered containers in the refrigerator.

If you own letter and number cookie cutters, try rolling out the fondant as directed above and cutting out a name to decorate the top of a special birthday cake.

Date Nut Balls

When my mother made these, I hated the job of chopping up the sticky dates. Now, fortunately, dates come already chopped in packages, and that takes all the work out of making these delightful confections. Several years ago, a good friend in Florida brought me some of these, rolled in coconut instead of confectioner's sugar, and I found it an interesting change. You may want to do some both ways for variety. At any rate, they're quick and easy to make and since they keep for weeks, tightly covered, they can be made before the worst holiday rush is upon you.

Makes 6 1/2 to 7 dozen balls, 3/4" in diameter

> 1/2 cup butter or margarine
> 1 8-ounce package chopped dates
> 1 cup pecans finely chopped
> 1 cup granulated sugar
> 1 1/2 cups Rice Krispies
> 2 teaspoons vanilla
> confectioner's sugar or flaked coconut

Melt butter in a heavy saucepan over low heat. Stir in dates, nuts and sugar and cook over medium heat (do not boil) for 8 minutes. Remove from heat; stir in vanilla and cereal bits. Cool until you can handle the mixture, but do not let it get completely cold. Pinch off small pieces and roll between the palms of your hand to form small balls, approximately 1/2"-3/4" in diameter. Roll in confectioner's sugar or flaked coconut and store in tightly covered containers.

Haystacks

This candy is good, quick and easy to make and relatively inexpensive, as candies go—all of which make it ideal for the busy holiday season. However, it has special nostalgic charm for me. In past years, when I worked a great deal with groups of children, I initiated countless youngsters, boys and girls, into the joy of candy-making with this simple recipe, and glowed inside as I watched the shiny-eyed look of pride as they packed small tins and trudged off home with a special gift "I made myself".

Makes 2 dozen

> 1 12-oz. package butterscotch candy bits
> 1 3-oz. can chow mein noodles
> 1/2 cup roasted unsalted peanuts, chopped fine (optional)

Melt candy bits in top of double boiler over hot, not boiling water. (As when melting chocolate, be careful that no water or steam gets into the candy.) Stir with a wooden spoon until smooth. Remove from heat. Stir in noodles and nuts, mixing well. Drop by teaspoonfuls onto waxed paper (this is the best time for the children to get into the act if they are helping you). Allow to harden completely before packing in tightly covered container.

Holly Wreaths

One of the most delightful women I've ever known taught me to make these. The wife of the minister of our small rural church, she was masterminding the annual Christmas caroling expedition of our church youngsters and I was helping. Each year, we helped the children make something that they could leave at the homes of the sick and elderly as they made their caroling rounds. One particular year, we decided on boxes of candy, and I set about finding the very easiest recipes possible. But none of mine equalled the success of these, which this amazing lady had even the most inept child turning out in a matter of minutes. Do try at least one batch. You'll be amazed at how "real" the holly wreaths look. And surprisingly enough, they're quite good to nibble on, too.

Makes 15 wreaths, approximately 2 1/2" in diameter

30 large marshmallows
1/2 cup butter of margarine
1/2 teaspoon vanilla extract
1 1/2 teaspoons green food coloring
3 1/2 cups corn flakes
Small red cinnamon candies for decoration

Melt marshmallows and butter over low heat in heavy saucepan. Beat slightly with wire whisk to be sure mixture is smooth. Stir in vanilla and food coloring and remove from heat. Stir in cornflakes. Using a tablespoon, drop onto wax paper, and using hands, mold into wreath shape. (Keep a damp cloth handy because this is a sticky job.) Add cinnamon dots for "holly berries". Allow to dry overnight before packing in tins. Use wax paper between each layer of wreaths.

Pecan-Mallow Puffs

When I was younger, I loved to travel anywhere that took us through Georgia because almost anywhere we stopped, there was a selection of delicious pecan candy for sale. My favorite was an airy, nut-and-caramel covered marshmallow confection, and I was always sorry when I'd eaten the last one. The memory of the taste drove me to experiment with a homemade version, which has turned out to be a success with all my friends. These are fun and easy to make—and have the added advantage of looking impressive.

Makes 3 dozen

> 18 large marshmallows, cut in half
> 1 12-ounce package vanilla caramels
> 1 tablespoon cream or condensed milk
> 1 1/2 teaspoons butter
> 8 ounces pecans, chopped finely

Cut marshmallows in half and set aside. In top of double boiler or in a heavy saucepan over low heat, melt caramels with cream and butter, stirring until mixture is smooth. Remove from heat. Drop a half of marshmallow into the caramel mixture. With a fork, roll it over until it is thoroughly coated. Lift out, allowing excess caramel to drip back into pan; roll in finely chopped pecans and place on wax paper to cool and dry. Repeat until all marshmallows have been dipped. When all are cool, wrap each piece individually in clear wrap and store in tightly covered container in a cool place.

Rocky Road

Almost every region of the country boasts one version of this candy as its "specialty". They're all similar, and all expensive to buy. In fact, the candy is relatively expensive to make because good chocolate comes high, but the ease of preparation plus the sinfully good finished product makes it money well spent. And nothing could please the true choc-o-holics on your Christmas list more. Wrapped in clear wrap or foil and stored in a cool place, it keeps well, so you can make it early. And it's versatile. Made in a disposable foil pan, it's a lovely gift with just the addition of a Christmas bow. Cut into small pieces, it can be packed in a gift container. Or molded 1 - 1½" deep in small loaf pans, it makes fantastic super-large candy bars for very special people.

Makes 1 9" x 9" square pan

> 1 lb. dark sweet chocolate
> 1 cup pecans broken into large pieces
> 12 large marshmallows cut in quarters or
>   48 miniature marshmallows

Break chocolate into small pieces and melt over hot, not boiling water, being careful not to get water or steam in the chocolate. In a buttered or foil-lined pan, pour half the chocolate. Arrange the nuts and marshmallows in a layer over the chocolate and cover with remaining half of the melted chocolate. If you are going to cut it into squares, score the block with a sharp knife after it sets slightly to give you guidelines for cutting when it is completely hardened. Allow to harden completely and either wrap with clear wrap or foil or cut in squares and pack in container.

Seafoam

In the depression years, the early thirties, most of the family grocery money was spent for necessities, so candy was a rare luxury and candy making was reserved for very special occasions. In our house, mother made candy only at Christmas. And my favorite was her Seafoam. Years later, when I think of holiday candy, I still think of Seafoam, and it was natural that it was one of the first recipes I tried when I started working on this book. I was disappointed when I tasted my first batch—it certainly did not measure up to memory. But it was my mother's recipe and it did look the way I remembered it, so I tried again. This time it tasted better and I began to realize that the melt-in-the-mouth sugary sweetness (almost too sweet to me after years of watching my weight) was the very thing that had made the candy a favorite of my childhood. It's relatively easy to make and it is pretty, but do save it for the real sweets lovers on your list.

Makes 4- 4 1/2 dozen pieces

> **3/4 cup water**
> **3 cups firmly packed light brown sugar**
> **1/4 teaspoon salt**
> **1/4 cup egg whites (usually 2)**
> **1 teaspoon vanilla**

Grease sides of saucepan. Cook water, sugar and salt over low heat, stirring constantly. Continue to cook until you cannot feel sugar grains when you rub your spoon against the side of the pan. Remove from heat and, with a damp cloth, carefully wipe off crystals on the sides of the pan. Place over medium heat and cover pan until mixture boils (2-3 minutes). Uncover and again wipe sugar crystals from sides of pan. Let mixture come back to a boil. Place candy thermometer in pan and cook over low heat, without stirring, until temperature registers 255° (hard ball stage). While syrup is boiling, beat egg whites until they stand in very stiff peaks. When syrup reaches desired temperature, pour it, in a small steady stream, into the egg whites, continuing to beat until all syrup is incorporated and candy no longer looks glossy. Drop a teaspoonful at a time quickly onto wax paper-lined cookie sheet. When completely cool and set, store in tightly covered container in cool dry place.